萬世師表

書畫中的孔子

Teacher Exemplar for a Myriad Generations

Confucius in Painting, Calligraphy, and Print Through the Ages

國立故宮博物院
NATIONAL PALACE MUSEUM

院長序

孔子被尊為「聖之時者」，意思是孔子的思想適用於各種時代。在崇尚國際化、現代化的二十一世紀，孔子的學行非但沒有被歷史塵封，反而突破時空，益發煥爛地成為西方世界樂於接受的潮流。尤其臺灣很早即受到聖賢的雨露霑溉，不論是傳統的學童啟蒙讀物《三字經》，或近年風行一時、以台語唱誦的《弟子規》，甚至高中文化基本教材的《論語》，都是孔子思想的結晶。可以說至今日，孔家儒學的價值資產依舊影響深遠，特別是東亞儒家文化圈。

孔子是史上偉大的教育家，享有「萬世師表」尊稱，其流傳後世的價值資產在於人文精神和教育理念，而孔子的教育主張「有教無類」與「因材施教」正擴大了教育的範圍，即所謂平民化的教育觀，應作為當代社會最重要的啟發。而博物館對大眾開放，期能為公眾所接近使用，亦為重要的社會教育場所，國立故宮博物院隨著漫漫歷史流淌，經過時代洗選所流傳下來的書畫藝術遺產中，自然保存了不少與孔子相關的

作品。以博物館的場域與文化脈絡重現古代儒門先哲的思想遺風，正是本院展出旨趣。

「萬世師表─書畫中的孔子」展覽規劃，嘗試突破早期以孔子學說作為禮教規訓的刻板印象，改以書畫藝術的視角，具體呈現孔子閒居、彈琴等生活化的面向，以及孔子所推崇的勇者卞莊子刺虎事蹟、門下弟子們的故事等等；展出書法部分，則有當今學習漢隸者熟知的〈乙瑛碑〉、〈禮器碑〉、〈史晨碑〉等，均是不同時期為了紀念孔子、或者紀錄修繕孔廟，製作出來傳諸後世的刻石與碑拓，至今均已成為廣受世人推重的書學範本。本院希望藉由此展，誠摯邀請大眾從書畫作品中再探孔子的思想與人生哲學，從中獲得學習資源。

國立故宮博物院 院長

林正儀

目次

4

展覽概述

康熙二十三年（一六八四），清聖祖南巡幸駕曲阜，親至闕里孔子故居，賜御筆「萬世師表」榜書，懸於大成殿中。翌年下詔摹搨此匾，頒發給天下文廟，「萬世師表」四字亦因此成為孔子的最佳代稱。而今，「萬世師表」也是全臺首學臺南孔廟大成殿內時代最早，面積最大的一塊匾額。

孔子（西元前五五一—西元前四四九）祖先為受封於宋國的殷商後裔，生於魯國，子姓，孔氏，名丘，字仲尼，後世敬稱孔子或孔夫子。他是東周時期的思想家與教育家，曾刪詩書，贊周易，訂禮樂，修春秋，成為後世科舉取士必讀教材，影響華夏文化至為深遠。鄰近的日本、韓國、越南以及東南亞等地區，亦受其學說霑溉，形成了儒家文化圈。

孔子被孟子尊為「聖之時者」，意思是其思想能適用於各個時代。孔子的言行、事蹟，與周遊列國的見聞，皆保存於《論語》、《孔子家語》，或散見於《史記》與諸子百家經史故事。本院書畫藏品中，頗多與孔子相關的作品。除了繪畫、版畫中的各類孔子肖像，書法中諸多漢隸名作、歷代碑刻、經典箴言，以及御筆書匾等，也都是漢代以來尊崇儒術所留下的歷史軌跡。本次共選展三十五組件，分「聖賢小像」、「刻碑崇聖」、「歷代尊儒」以及「經典圖繪」等四個單元，援以向這位數千年來，以聖德雨露滋養華夏文化的萬世師表致敬。

6

一 聖賢小像

孔子晚年雖然已成王者之師，但最早為孔子畫像塑形的記載，見於《後漢書·蔡邕傳》，直到東漢靈帝光和元年（一七八），置鴻都門學，方畫孔子及七十二弟子像，時間比孔子在世時晚了六百多年。今日所見，各種各樣已成既定印象的孔子繪圖，其實泰半出於後人根據文獻描述的揣摩和想像。

大成至聖文宣王

1 至聖先賢半身像 孔子

全冊六十開,圖繪起自孔子,終
至許衡（一二○九－一二八一）,自
春秋（前七七○－前四七六）至元代
一百二十位歷代名儒,原在清宮安奉
歷代帝后賢臣圖像的「南薰殿」。

按題籤封號,可知繪製時間在元
文宗至順元年（一三三○）追封孔子
各大弟子公爵之位以後。本次選展為
首以孔門四配十哲順序裝裱的七開,
十哲見《論語‧先進第十一》,孔子
自言孔門四科之佳者德行：顏淵、閔
子騫、冉伯牛、仲弓。言語：宰我、
子貢。政事：冉有、季路。文學：子
游、子夏。四配之例則成於南宋度宗
咸淳三年（一二六七）,以顏淵、曾參、
孔伋、孟軻配饗。

兗國復聖公 顏回 子淵

2 至聖先賢半身像 顏回

顏回（西元前五二一—前四八一），字子淵，又稱顏子、顏淵，魯國人。少孔子三十歲，其人寡言好學，不遷怒、不貳過，安貧樂道，孔門十哲德行之首，被視作孔子最得意的弟子。年四十一歲而卒，孔子哀之甚慟。三國魏正始二年（二四一）少帝詔「以顏淵配」，是孔門最早被列入配享的弟子。唐玄宗開元二十七年（三七九）追封「兗公」，元文宗至順元年（一三三〇）又加封「兗國復聖公」。

郕國宗聖公　曾參 子輿

3 至聖先賢半身像　曾參

曾參（西元前五〇五—前四三五），
字子輿，後世稱曾子，魯國武城（今山
東費縣）人。少孔子四十六歲，其父
曾點亦孔子門生。曾參以孝見稱，歸
納孔子一以貫之之道為「忠恕」二字，
提出「吾日三省吾身」的修養模式，
為孔子孫孔伋之師。自唐高宗總章元
年（六六八）始有封贈，為「太子少
保」。南宋度宗咸淳三年（一二六七）
升列配享行列，題籤「郕國宗聖公」
為元文宗至順元年（一三三〇）所加
封。

沂國述聖公　孔伋　子思

至聖先賢半身像　孔伋

4

孔伋（西元前四八三～前四〇二），字子思，有「述聖」之稱，為孔子之孫，孔鯉（西元前五三二～前四八三）之子，曾受業於曾子，相傳孟子曾師從在其弟子門下。著有《子思子》，流傳至今者僅《中庸》，主張維持中和，避免偏頗太過，追求「至誠」，以為修身養性之理。宋徽宗封孔伋為「沂水侯」，元文宗封「沂國述聖公」，與「復聖」顏回、「宗聖」曾參、「亞聖」孟軻並稱四配。

鄒國亞聖公 孟軻

至聖先賢半身像 孟軻

5

孟軻（西元前三七二―前二八九），世稱孟子，鄒國（今山東鄒城）人。戰國儒家代表人物。主要思想有民本、仁義等政治理論與性善論。自唐代韓愈（七六八―八二四）著〈原道〉，以孟子為先秦唯一繼承孔子道統者後，地位逐漸超越顏回。宋神宗熙寧四年（一〇七一）首次列《孟子》為科舉項目，元豐六年（一〇八三）封「鄒國公」，翌年准配享孔廟。南宋將《孟子》列入四書，實際地位更在五經之上。

費公閔 損 子騫

至聖先賢半身像 閔損

6

閔損（前五三六－前四八七），字子騫，魯人。孔門十哲之一，少孔子十五歲，以德行修養著稱。孔子評其：「夫人不言，言必有中。」可知子騫，人不言，言必有中。孔子又贊：「孝哉！閔子騫，人不間於其父母昆弟之間。」為《二十四孝》中〈單衣順母〉故事的主角。《論語·雍也第六》載閔損不滿季氏，辭費宰之使，然後世多封閔損在費，唐封費侯，宋封費公，似欲彰顯己朝無季氏專擅之弊。

郿公冉 耕 伯牛

7 至聖先賢半身像 冉耕

冉耕（前五四四-？），字伯牛，與冉雍同宗，魯人。少孔子七歲，染惡疾早逝。十哲之一，以德行著稱，孔子任司寇時，以冉耕為中都宰。關於其人記載甚少，卒年不詳。

據孔門四科十哲由來的《論語·先進第十一》：「子曰：『從我於陳蔡者，皆不及門也。』德行：顏淵、閔子騫、冉伯牛、仲弓；言語：宰我、子貢；政事：冉有、季路；文學：子游、子夏。」僅知亦曾從孔子周遊列國。

薛公冉 雍 仲弓

至聖先賢半身像 冉雍

8

冉雍（前五二一—？），字仲弓，魯人。少孔子二十九歲。唐贈薛侯，宋封下邳公，改封薛公。生於不肖之父。為人篤實慮深，氣度寬宏，以德行著稱，亦長於政事。魯哀公十三年（前四八二），即隨孔子周遊列國回魯之後第三年，冉雍嘗事季桓子（？—前四九二），為季氏宰，時年四十一歲。在《論語》中，冉雍曾數度問政、問仁，孔子贊其「可使南面」，有人君之度。

齊公宰 予 子我

至聖先賢半身像 宰予

宰予（前五二二—前四五八），字子我，又稱宰我，魯人。孔門十哲之一，少孔子二十九歲，擅長辭令，是《論語》中最常因驚人之語被孔子責備的學生。最著名者為其晝寢，其次是問可否縮短父母三年之喪為一年，被孔子痛斥不仁。然孟子認為宰我極敬孔子，且「智足以知聖人」。或因其思想活躍，為人自信，常對孔子提出異議，故予《論語》編者留下如此印象。

黎公端木 賜 子貢

至聖先賢半身像 端木賜

10

端木賜（前五二〇－前四四六），字子貢，衞人。少孔子三十一歲，以言語聞名。孔子的得意門生，曾稱其為「瑚璉之器」。其人擅雄辯，有幹才，曾任魯、衞諸國之相，遊說吳國出師制齊以存魯，在外交方面成就斐然；並長於經商，為孔門弟子首富。孔子死後，子貢廬墓六年，為他人之倍，弘揚孔子學說極力。從《論語》對其記載，可推測子貢及其門徒是編成《論語》的重要力量。

徐公冉 求 子有

至聖先賢半身像 冉求

冉求（前五二一－？），字子有，
亦稱冉有，魯人。少孔子二十九歲。
《論語・憲問》孔子答子路成人之問，
曾以冉求之藝與臧武仲之智、孟公綽
之不欲和卞莊子之勇並列。冉求為人
謙讓退縮多才藝，以政事著名。曾為
季康子（？－前四六八）家宰，對孔
子晚年歸隱魯國出力甚多。因替季氏
聚斂徵稅，加上無法攔阻季氏僭禮祭
泰山而受責，冉求的處境亦反映了孔
子的間接政治影響力。

衞公仲由字子路

至聖先賢半身像 仲由

12

仲由（前五四二─前四八〇），字子路，或稱季路，魯國卞人。少孔子九歲，是弟子中侍奉孔子最久者。除學詩、禮外，還為孔子趕車，護衞孔子周遊列國。為人伉直魯莽，好勇力，重然諾，且忠於職守。事親至孝，為《二十四孝》中為親負米故事的主角。子路長於政事，初仕魯，後事衞。曾為季氏宰，後任衞大夫孔悝家臣，為護主死難於衞。唐代追封為「衞侯」，南宋進封「衞公」。

吳公言偃 子游

至聖先賢半身像 言偃

13

言偃（前五〇六—前四四三），字子游，亦稱言游，文稱叔氏，吳人。少孔子四十五歲，是孔子七十二弟子中唯一的南方人。以文學著名，曾任魯國武城（曾參家鄉，今山東費縣）宰，以禮樂教育士民，境內遍有弦歌之聲，博得孔子讚賞。後學成南歸，道啟東南，對江南文化繁榮有很大貢獻，被譽為「南方夫子」，尊稱言子。唐開元年間封「吳侯」，宋封「丹陽公」，後又稱「吳公」。

22

魏公卜商　子夏

至聖先賢半身像　卜商

14

卜商（前五〇七─？），字子夏。家貧勤學，孔門十哲，長於文學，孔子逝後曾執教於魏國西河（今陝西渭南），為魏文侯師。晚年喪子，哭而失明，為曾子所責。孔門弟子之有著作傳世者，以子夏為最多。相傳《毛詩》傳自子夏，《詩序》為子夏所作，《儀禮·喪服篇》傳自子夏，《易傳》一卷亦子夏所撰，孔門傳經之勤，首推子夏，可見其在孔門地位之重要。

宋 高宗書孝經 馬和之繪圖

孝經全文共十八章，據說是曾子（前五〇五－前四三五）問孝於孔子，由曾子學生們記載而成的一部書。將社會上各階層人士，分為上自國家元首，下至平民百姓等五個層級，標示其實踐孝道的法則與途徑。本幅選自《宋人書畫孝經冊》第一開，繪孔子居中講學，曾子長跪問孝。推測原為圖文相連的長卷，後因破損改裝成書畫分開的冊頁形式。全冊圖文相輔，畫幅各藉不同場景，詮釋各階層人士盡孝及忠君的雙重意涵，充分突顯了「為君主立言」的創作初衷。本冊書風略似高宗，應是御書院書手代筆。畫幅風格與馬和之不同，實為宋人託名之作。

開宗明義章第一

仲尼居曾子侍子曰先王有至德要道以順天下民用
和睦上下無怨汝知之乎曾子避席曰參不敏何足以
知之子曰夫孝德之本也教之所由生也復坐吾語汝
身體髮膚受之父母不敢毀傷孝之始也立身行道揚
名於後世以顯父母孝之終也夫孝始於　親中於

中原懷復志曾氣如云風鬱四方動

教孝經成書

抑是頌乎抑刺乎

豈冊舊稱馬和之繪圖已入石渠寶笈上等今以義
暇重觀冊後讀人所識皆以為高宗書詔畫苑設像
立儀且冊中都無馬和之名則成書時屬之和之去
乃失於考證也阮也成書因書冊中以識決疑求是
之言玉於訣人舉嘉陵以孝治天下中興之主達於
中國四方嚮風云云言過其實夫高宗被金源
所逼偃偓保江南又不能復中原近二章第斯數語能
毋汗顏乎歲之以存乞論

癸巳新春下澣涵芬筆

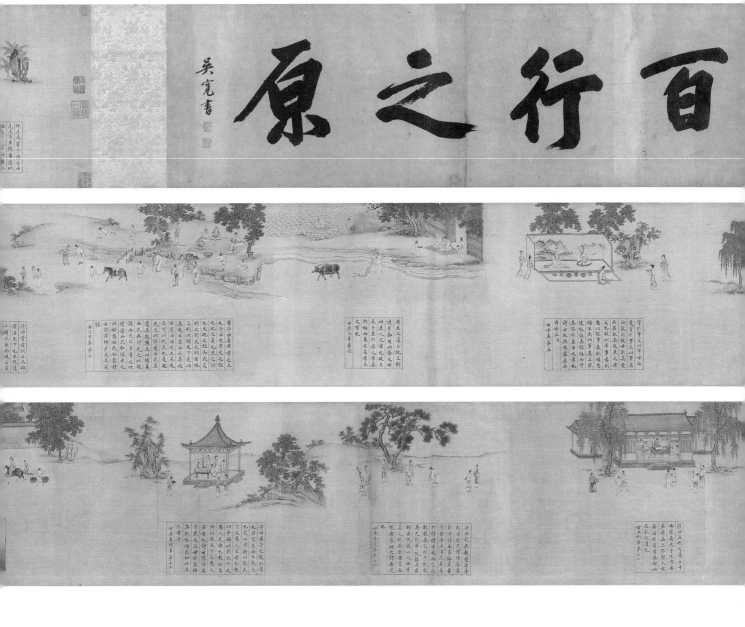

明 文徵明楷書孝經 仇英畫

文徵明（一四七○－一五五九），
江蘇長洲人，文人畫家，書畫兼擅，
書法以小楷及小行草成就最高。仇英
（約西元一四九四－一五五二），江
蘇太倉人，字實父，號十洲，職業畫
家，畫風細膩雅致。

《孝經》全文僅一千八百多字，
出於儒家對孝道的重視，成為十三經
中字數最少的一經。本卷打破宋代左
圖右文形式，以孔子與諸弟子杏壇講
學始，接連描繪《孝經》十八章，用
筆剛勁簡練。據嘉靖丙午（一五四六）
文氏跋，仇英此畫摹北宋王端（約活
動於一○○四－一○二三）孝經圖，
完成後藏家王作賓復請文氏楷書文字
於畫下，成為書畫合璧之作。

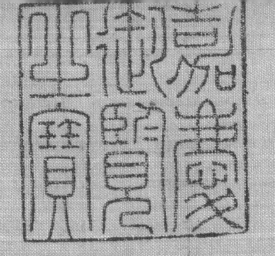

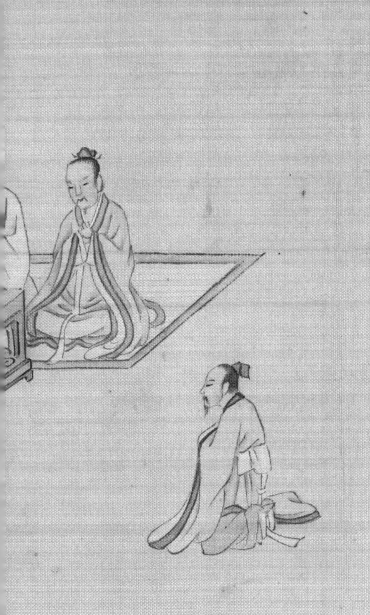

宋人　畫歷代琴式圖

古琴，亦稱七弦琴，中國最古老的彈撥樂器之一，孔子時代即已盛行，創製者有「伏羲作琴」、「神農作琴」與「舜作五弦之琴」等說，琴式命名的方式，反映了古人對聖賢、帝王和文人的推崇。本冊原貯於清代太子所居之重華宮，舊傳為宋人所作，以水墨畫歷代帝王與古聖賢琴式，每幅上方並錄相關故實一則，共計三十一幅，本次選展〈老聃之制〉與〈孔子之制〉，在齊聞韶，三月不知肉味的孔子愛樂，眾人皆知。琴體腰與頸部方折凹入，通體線條流暢的仲尼琴式，是唐宋以來最常見的古琴種類，至今依舊是最為流行的古琴款式。但就畫風判斷，應為明人摹本。

孔子之製
孔子父叔梁紇
與顏氏禱於尼
山而生孔子未
生時母見麒麟
嚙玉書吐於闕
里異之乃以绣
紱繫麟角信宿
而去懷娠十二
月而生兒時嬉
戲嘗陳俎豆設
禮容長為季氏
史問禮於老子
之後而莘子稍
益進尊周之禮
樂製琴長三尺
六寸四分亦用
周之尺也

老子

聖君賢臣全身像 老子 孔子

本冊以絹本水墨繪自伏羲至
唐德宗（七四二─八○五）等五代
（九○七─九六○）以前帝王與聖
賢名士全身肖像共四十六幅，畫風
類似大英博物館〈女史箴圖〉宋摹
本，而線條更加直接精簡。本次選
展第十七開，畫老子及孔子，線條
勻稱，流暢細勁，衣褶以墨暈染，
意甚高古。《史記·孔子世家》記
魯君與孔子適周問禮，老子曰：「吾
聞富貴者送人以財，仁人者送人以
言。吾不能富貴，竊仁人之號，送
子以言，曰：『聰明深察而近於死
者，好議人者也。博辯廣大危其身
者，發人之惡者也。為人子者毋以
有己，為人臣者毋以有己。』」是
「孔子見老子」故事發源。

46

孔子

聖廟祀典圖攷卷一　長洲顧沅湘舟敬輯

清　聖廟祀典圖攷　至聖先師孔子像

19

〈至聖先師孔子像〉線描版畫，繪孔子濃眉豐髯，冠服端整，持笏正坐。由手勢與面部張口露齒的表情推測，所繪應為《論語·鄉黨》所記孔子「其在宗廟朝廷，便便言，唯謹爾」之言貌。孔子持物見《禮記·玉藻》：「笏，天子以球玉，諸侯以象，大夫以魚須文竹，士竹，本，象可也……凡有指畫於君前，用笏；造受命於君前，則書於笏。笏，畢用也，因飾焉。」依古禮制，諸侯士大夫須持笏見天子，在天子面前若需指畫，則以笏為之。本幅所繪為孔子在廟堂之上為天子陳述政事的情形，線條類似高古游絲描，筆筆均勻細勁。對開文字為自周至隋歷代帝王對孔子的追封。

孔子　諱口字仲尼出處事實詳聖迹圖　周敬

王四十二年魯哀公諱之曰尼父　鄭康成謂因字

之卽舊宅立廟令世世以歲時祀孔子家漢高帝

十二年過魯以太牢祀孔子　後世帝王祀孔子始此

始元年追諡褒成宣尼公　諡實東漢明帝永平二

年命辟雍及郡縣學校皆祀孔子　國學郡縣祀孔子始此

魏孝文帝太和十六年改諡文聖尼父北齊之制

每歲春秋二仲釋奠每月旦朔日行禮始此　後世春秋釋奠北

周宣帝大象二年追封鄒國公隋文帝時諡先師

聖賢像贊卷

宋太祖建隆三年御製贊
惟帝王取則堯舜
則吾夫子其集大成
功茂德實
名垂萬世
河海標墨
鳳鳴岐陽
其儀不忒
東西南北

宋真宗御製贊
人倫之表
儒術所宗
群哲之揆
百世之師
立人之道
云誰不崇

宋仁宗御製贊
訓述詩定禮
盛典聿揚
哲人既生
巍巍尼父
其用不窮

宋徽宗御製贊
厥初生民
乃有聖德
斯文在茲
古今之師
巍巍尼父
今古共崇

宋高宗御製贊
乃有嚴祖
道山德海
大哉宣王
道山德海
甘月共明
海宇津崇

宋理宗御製贊
大哉宣尼
戰戰在春秋載籍
此武功
肅昭盛德
日月昭回

崇寧
聖薇尼父
宋理宗紹定三年御製
虛聘列國
道大莫容

至聖先師孔子 名丘字 仲尼此
東兗州鄒曲阜縣人

20

明　聖賢像贊　至聖先師孔子

明呂維祺（一五八七－一六四一）
輯，崇禎間（一六二八－一六四四）刊版，
此本「玄」字缺末點，推測刷印時間已至
康熙朝。《至聖先師孔子》繪身形魁梧的
孔子頭戴儒巾，鬚眉豐茂，雙手持笏，正
坐直視前方，意態端嚴，精神奕奕。線條
明快剛勁，風格質樸，以對比鮮明的大面
積黑色色塊處理孔子袍服，並用留白法處
理袍袖摺紋。

呂維祺，字介孺，新安（今河南）
人。明代理學家，河南名儒呂孔學之
子。呂維祺自幼習理學，萬曆四十一年
（一六一三）進士，授兗州推官，擢
吏部主事。因得罪魏忠賢（一五六八－
一六二七），辭官還鄉，設芝泉講會。崇
禎間復官，任南京兵部尚書，李自成攻陷
洛陽，被俘不屈而死。諡忠節，清朝諡忠
敬。

至聖先師孔子

東兗州府曲阜縣人

仲尼山

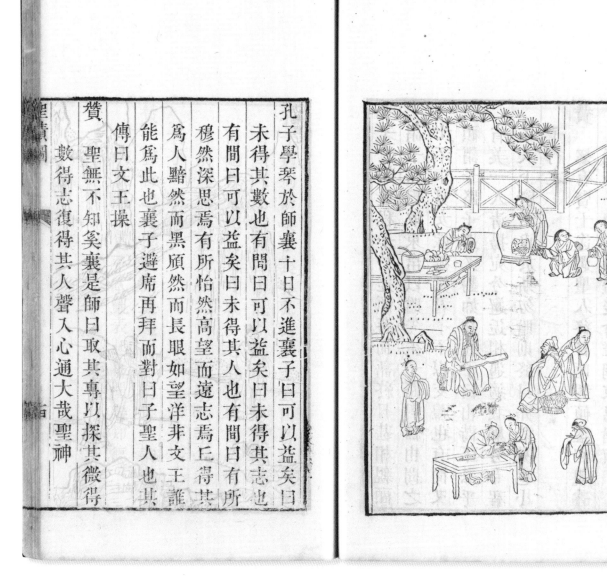

孔子學琴於師襄十日不進襄子曰可以益矣曰
未得其數也有間曰可以益矣曰未得其志也
有間曰可以益矣曰未得其人也有間曰有所
穆然深思焉有所怡然高望而遠志焉曰得其
爲人黯然而黑頎然而長眼如望羊洋非文王誰
能爲此也襄子避席再拜而對曰子聖人也其
傳曰文王操

贊

聖無不知奚是師曰取其專以探其微得
數得志復得其人聲入心通大哉聖神

清　聖廟祀典圖攷　學琴師襄

《聖廟祀典圖攷》共五卷，以清
代頒定從祀位次為準，收錄孔子、孔
子弟子及歷代名儒，自漢至清歷代配
祀孔廟者一百四十四人畫像與小傳。

編者顧沅（一七九九－一八五一），
字湘舟，長洲（今蘇州）人。道光間曾
官教諭，為著名藏書家，著述編刻宏富。
繪圖者孔繼堯，字硯香，號蓮鄉，江蘇
昆山人，善刻花鳥，尤工人物，顧氏之
書多由其摹繪畫像。

此為道光六年（一八二六）顧沅
「賜硯堂」刊本，歷代多繪孔子生平
為《聖蹟圖》，本開《學琴師襄》為
卷五孔子向樂官師襄子學琴故事，圖
文相輔，講述孔子必求甚解的學習精
神，以線刻版畫印孔子松下挽袖鼓琴，
狀甚投入。

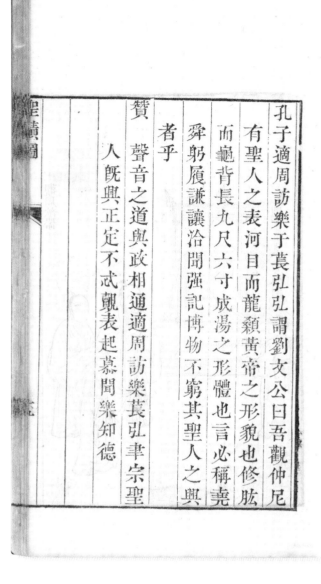

孔子適周訪樂于萇弘弘謂劉文公曰吾觀仲尼

有聖人之表河目而龍顙黃帝之形貌也修肱

而龜背長九尺六寸成湯之形體也言必稱堯

舜躬履謙讓洽聞強記博物不窮其聖人之興

者乎

　贊

　聲音之道與政相通適周訪樂萇弘韋宗聖

人既與正定不忒覬表起慕聞樂知德

清 聖廟祀典圖敬 訪樂萇弘

22

萇弘（?—前四九二），東周蜀（今四川資中縣）人，著名學者與政治家，通曉天文曆數與音律、樂理。《史記·封禪書》載：「萇弘以方事周靈王。」是周天子諮詢星象吉凶與各種徵兆問題的顧問對象。

本開《訪樂萇弘》所繪，為周敬王二十四至二十五年間（前四九六—前四九五），孔子拜訪萇弘，請教音樂問題的故事。對開文字敘述乃傳說中，以見微知著聞名的萇弘，向他人表達自己觀察孔子外表，發現各種與古代聖賢相同特徵的敘述。

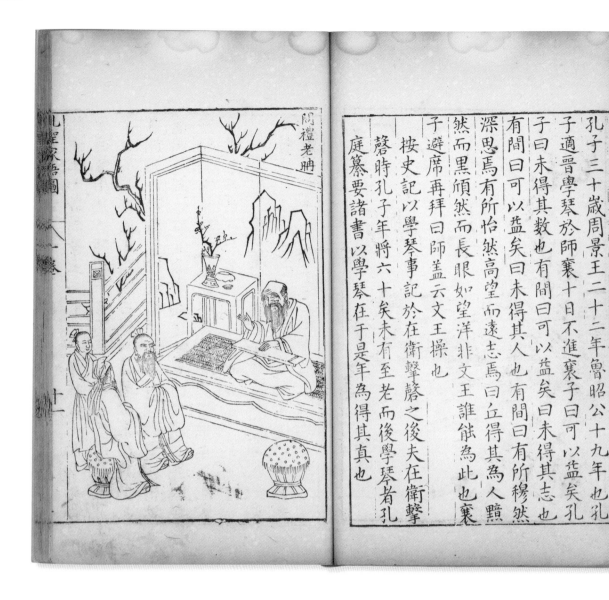

孔子三十歲周景王二十二年魯昭公十九年也孔
子適晉學琴於師襄十日不進襄子曰可以益矣孔
子曰未得其數也有間曰可以益矣曰未得其志也
有間曰可以益矣曰未得其人也有間曰有所穆然
深思焉有所怡然高望而遠志焉曰丘得其為人黯
然而黑頎然而長眼如望洋非文王誰能為此也襄
子避席再拜曰師蓋云文王操也

按史記以學琴事記於在衛擊磬之後夫在衛擊
磬時孔子年將六十矣未有至老而後學琴者孔
庭纂要諸書以學琴在于是年為得其真也

明 孔聖家語圖 問禮老聃

23

《孔聖家語圖》，明吳嘉謨據曲阜《聖
跡圖》為藍本，萬曆十七年（一五八九
）集校刻印，程起龍伯陽甫繪寫，歙人黃
組鐫刻。共十一卷，卷二至十為《孔子
家語》文字，卷一為孔子一生自誕生到
逝世之聖蹟圖繪，共四十幅，對幅為與
圖參照之傳文及按語。版畫圖版面簡
潔，構圖勻稱，線條流暢，刀法粗獷，
注重繪刻人物神態表情。

早在東漢畫像石中，〈問禮老聃〉
即是相當常見的主題。《禮記·曾子問》、
《史記·老子韓非子列傳》、《孔子世家》
及《莊子》等書均有「孔子問禮於老子」
相關記載。

問禮老聃

二 刻碑崇聖

孔子逝世之後，歷代帝王與地方官員追封祭祀孔子、修築孔廟皆刻石立碑以誌其事。撰文書碑者皆為當代文壇書壇的一時之選，久而久之，形成了盛名遠播的碑林，其中如〈乙瑛碑〉、〈禮器碑〉、〈史晨碑〉等均為漢隸傑作，為今日的書法愛好者，留下諸多值得師法仿效的名品。

漢 乙瑛碑

24

〈乙瑛碑〉，東漢永興元年（一五三）立。碑文記載孔子十九世孫孔麟，請求依照漢代祠廟定制，設立百石卒史，負責孔廟禮器、春秋祭典各項禮儀。事經魯前相乙瑛、後相平，以及司徒吳雄、司空趙戒先後奏聞，終得賢者孔龢，以學德兼備、事親至孝，獲選充任此事。碑文隸書，原碑在山東曲阜，又稱「孔龢碑」，目前安置於曲阜孔廟。清人推為漢隸典型，是最多人師法端謹肅穆，沉厚雍容，的隸書範本之一。

此碑除廟方執事人員外，數度提及「出王家錢給犬酒」，「河南尹給牛羊豕雞□□各一。大司農給米」，可為孔廟草創期祭品的參考資料。

信曹月桓王畫

持立廟德父樂

出王家纂室犬

孫大軍總

天子大言孔天大

如王高孔安

司徒吏雒司空吏奏稽首言並廟用
驛徑律天地宗神饗明故楅玉家廟
入主朝地泰畤措神禮出楅
行無夫聖附奉世正故玉
大于司農文祠猪者子財此玉
日如故事更宋祠里愚以孔禮子吞
可事更雒明祠里博愚子羲謂如子城
日可雒里宗傳以人孔誠可斑
三十事愚趙罰如稈子吞天
嘉二月更日宬計宮

元嘉三年□□三月□奉于邦□□七□禮日□六

軺雜詠利朓六□□聖□□□

永興元年□月甲辰朔十八日孔子□廟□

司空府□王寅詔書□□元朝□

□奏□□司宗府遣者平邦頭邦孔子□

春殿□尺□□通高□兼事親至孝朕

諸曰□王現府魏大聖共共彌章相□

□君宗榮守宅□□史孔子十九□

釋文：

司徒臣雄。司空臣戒。稽首言。魯前相瑛書言。詔書崇聖道。勉學藝。孔子作春秋。制孝經。刪述五經。演易繫

辭。經緯天地。幽讚神明。故特立廟。褒成侯四時來祠。事已即去。廟有禮器。無常人掌領。請置百石卒史一

人。典主守廟。春秋饗禮。財出王家錢。給犬酒直。須報。謹問大常祠曹掾馮牟。史郭玄辭對。故事辟雍禮未

行。祠先聖師。侍祠者孔子子孫。大宰。大祝。令各一人。皆備爵。大常丞監祠。河南尹給牛羊豕雞□□各一。

大司農給米祠。臣愚以為。如瑛言。孔子大聖。則象乾坤。為漢制作。先世所尊。祠用眾牲。常吏備爵。今欲加

寵子孫。敬恭明祀。傳于罔極。可許臣請。魯相為孔子廟置百石卒史一人。掌領禮器。出王家錢。給犬酒直。

他如故事。臣雄臣戒愚戇。誠惶誠恐。頓首頓首。死罪死罪。臣稽首以聞。致

曰可。司徒公河南原武吳雄字季高。

元嘉三年三月廿七日壬寅。奏雒陽宮。司空工蜀郡成都趙戒字意伯。

元嘉三年三月丙子朔。廿七日壬寅。司徒雄司空戒。下魯相承書從事。下當用者。選其年卌以上。經通一

藝。雜試通利。能奉弘先聖之禮。為宗所歸者。如詔書。書到言。

永興元年六月甲辰朔十八日辛酉。魯相平行長史事。卞守長擅。叩頭死罪。敢言之。

司徒司空府壬寅詔書。為孔子廟置百石卒史一人。掌主禮器。選年卌以上。經通一藝。雜試能奉弘先聖

之禮。為宗所歸者。平叩頭叩頭。死罪死罪。謹案文書。守文學掾魯孔龢。師孔憲。戶曹史孔覽等。雜試龢脩

春秋嚴氏。經通高第。事親至孝。能奉先聖之禮。為宗所歸。除龢補名狀如牒。平惶恐叩頭。死罪死罪。上

司空府

讚曰。巍巍大聖。赫赫彌章。相乙瑛字少卿。平原高唐人。令鮑疊字文公。上黨屯留人。政教稽古。若重規矩。

乙君察舉守宅除吏。孔子十九世孫麟。廉請置百石卒史一人。鮑君造作百石吏舍。功垂无窮。於是始□。

司徒臣雄司空臣奏稽首言魯前相瑛書言諸書崇聖道
群律典主朝廷天地圖讀神明廟恩四時未河事已即奉
農大夫卜侍恭父卜侍孔子元後復明故犆立廟恩二
如故事臣雄臣戒愚以為如孔子大聖則土宜王家
可雜里禮儀為里戎傳子孔子大祝令各一人給犬酒
自嘉三年六月舍嘉言誠惶誠恐頓首死罪死罪頓
元嘉三年三月乙丑朔廿七日壬寅雒陽宮
元興元年試元未六月用辰朝廿一日乙酉雒陽宮諸
永興司空府諸書到言諸書到諸書相
永興司空府如詔書諸書言
司徒府諸書守文守禮宗所聖
春卒史孔嵩乎邛頭孔子宅守文守禮宗所聖
司空府諸君親至孔子宅守文守禮宗所聖
日記現大聖共禰軍相人璞字少卿平原高唐人令鮑
諸君曰記現大聖共禰軍相人璞字少卿平原高唐人令鮑
君來守宅府奉孔子十九世孫麟字文遠上臺年古

漢 禮器碑

25

〈禮器碑〉，全稱〈漢魯相韓敕造孔廟禮器碑〉，又名〈韓敕碑〉、〈修孔子廟器碑〉等，東漢永壽二年（一五六）刻，與〈乙瑛〉、〈史晨〉合稱廟堂三巨制。

碑文記述魯相韓敕修整孔廟、置辦禮器，和吏民共同捐資立石頌德之事。此碑為東漢碑刻書法經典之作，字口完整，運筆變化多端，書風細勁雄健，端嚴峻逸，結體和諧穩健，整體神采超然，秀雅肅穆。工漢隸者多以其縱橫跌宕為楷模，對後世影響深遠。

此碑述及孔子母族顏氏與妻族「并官氏」，目前常見孔子妻「亓官氏」資料，但宋代《通志》與明以前姓氏考證類書則均為「并官氏」。

惟永壽二年。青龍在渻。歎霜月之靈。皇極之日。魯相。河南京。韓君。追惟大古。華胥生皇雄。顏□

育孔寶。俱制元道。百王不改。孔子近聖。為漢定道。自天王以下。至于初學。莫不驅思嘆仰師鏡。

顏氏聖舅。家居魯親里。并官聖妃。在安樂里。聖族之親。禮所宜異。復顏氏。邑中繇發。以

尊孔心。念聖歷世。禮樂陵遲。秦項作亂。不尊圖書。倍道畔德。離敗聖輿。食糧。亡于沙丘。君於是

造立禮器。樂之音符。鍾磬瑟鼓。雷洗觴觚。爵鹿柤椫。籩柉禁壺。脩飾宅廟。更作二輿。朝車威熹。

宣抒玄汙。以注水流。法舊不煩。備而不奢。上合紫臺。稽之中和。下合聖制。事得禮儀。於是四方

土仁。聞君風燿。敬咏其德。尊琦大人之意。違彊之思。乃共立表石。紀傳億載。其文曰。□

皇戲統華胥。承天畫卦。顏育空桑。孔制元孝。俱祖紫宮。大一所授。前闓九頭。以斗言教。後制百王。

獲麟來吐。制不空作。承天之語。乾元以來。三九之載。八皇三代。至孔乃備。聖人不世。期五百載。

三陽吐圖。二陰出讖。制作之義。以俟知奧。於穆韓君。獨見天意。復聖二族。違越絕思。脩造禮樂。

胡輦器用。存古舊宇。愍勳宅廟。朝車威熹。出誠造□。漆不水解。工不爭賈。深除玄汙。水通四注。

禮器升堂。天雨降澍。百姓訢和。舉國蒙慶。神靈祐誠。竭敬之報。天與厥福。永享牟壽。上極華紫。

旁伎皇代。刊石表銘。與乾運燿。長期蕩蕩。於盛復授。赫赫罔窮。聲垂億載。

韓明府名勑字叔節。故涿郡大守。魯。麃次公。五千。故從事。魯。張。嵩。眇高。五百。

潁川長社。王玄。君真。二百。故會稽大守。魯。傅世起。千。相主薄。魯。薛陶元方。三百。

河東大陽。西門儉。元節。二百。故樂安相。魯。麃公。千。相史。魯。周乾。伯德。三百。

漢 史晨碑

26

〈史晨碑〉，現存曲阜孔廟，兩面刻石，碑陰稱〈史晨後碑〉，東漢靈帝建寧元年（一六八）刻，述魯相史晨修護孔廟事；碑陽稱〈史晨前碑〉，建寧二年（一六九）刻，記史晨到官時拜祭孔子，並上書奏請每年春秋兩季行祭孔禮之事。此碑前後書風相類，似同出一人之手，文字磨滅極少。字體中宮緊縮，波磔開張，布白均勻，筆法溫和蘊藉，氣勢肅括宏深，沉古遒厚，法度森嚴，結構與意度皆備，為東漢隸碑傑作。

後碑所述之「河東大守孔彪元上」，即顏書所祖〈孔彪碑〉碑主；亦是〈孔宙碑〉碑主孔融父孔宙之弟，均為孔子聖裔，可見其族人材輩出。

禮義馬泰王稽儀廟

稠乳子夫宰長吏非

以祈罪曰令祀百

闕不不祀誠亦

臣復息死情思惟

上首頓首死罔死罔臣盡

建寧二年三月癸
荷書史晨頓首頓首
壹憂乳辱夏頌眾頓首
復禪孔子宅拜謁神
以奉錢俯上宗食敢
王天申己王亥昧

史晨前碑

頃穿伯時徙越騎校尉拜建

踰更公既從　堂扉軹春拜公

無胝公出享至勒羨銖固本悲

李諱賻刊獻銘并列自　春父

酮故敬讓五宜疾魯孔暢　文

塙尚書孔立元世河孔列攷孚

邪字庚倮來觀無晔宜東終曰

又　五　舞　目果　　大

洙請曰墅航蕃補完車以斗

恐縣夾緞民侵掔百姓酤賈自

災共去市道遠百姓

芳治桐車馬於瀆上東行道

開舍及魯公冢守吏凡四人

漢　史晨前碑

釋文：

建寧二年三月癸卯朔七日己酉。魯相臣晨。長史臣謙頓首死罪上

尚書。臣晨頓首頓首。死罪死罪。臣蒙厚恩。受任符守。得在奎妻。周孔舊寓。不能闡弘德政。恢崇

壹變。夙夜憂怖。累息屏營。臣晨頓首頓首。死罪死罪。臣以建寧元年到官。行秋饗。飲酒畔宮。畢。

復禮孔子宅。拜謁神坐。仰瞻槐楎。俯視几筵。靈所馮依。肅肅猶存。而無公出酒脯之祠。臣即自

以奉錢。脩上案食醊具。以敘小節。不敢空謁。臣伏念孔子。乾坤所挺。西狩獲麟。為漢制作。故孝

經援神挈曰。玄丘制命帝卯行。又尚書考靈耀曰。丘生倉際。觸期稽度為赤制。故作春秋。以明

文命。綴紀撰書。修定禮義。臣以為素王稽古。德亞皇代。雖有褒成世享之封。四時來祭畢。即歸

國。臣伏見。臨璧雍日。祠孔子以大牢。長吏備爵。所以尊先師重教化也。夫封土為社。立稷而祀。

皆為百姓興利除害。以祈豐穰。月令祀百辟卿士有益於民。矧乃孔子。玄德煥炳。光於上下。而

本國舊居。復禮之日。闕而不祀。誠

朝廷聖恩所宜特加。臣寢息耿耿。情所思惟。臣輒依社稷出王家穀春秋行禮。以共煙祀。餘脯

賜先生執事。臣晨頓首頓首。死罪死罪。臣盡力思惟庶政。報稱為效。增異輒上。臣晨誠惶誠恐。

頓首頓首。死罪死罪。上

尚書。時副言大傳。大尉。司徒。司空。大司農府治所部從事。

昔在仲尼。汁光之精。大帝所挺。顏母毓靈。承敝遭衰。黑不代倉。周流應聘。歎鳳不臻。自衛反魯。

養徒三千。獲麟趣作。端門見徵。血書著紀。黃玉響應。主為漢制。道審可行。乃作春秋。複演孝經。

刪定六藝。象與天談。鉤河摘雒。卻揆未然。魏魏蕩蕩。與乾比崇。

建寧二年三月

尚書臣晨頓首頓首死罪臣晨長史文

掾臣豪頓首死罪長吏文

緣奉橚禋禋子上宅夏頌頴旱

政績九成夫人

文綉臣晨頓首上書謹按

國國為臣伏見

國舊居延見興邸禮廟

先聖執事以時霜露之時

頌首頓首死罪臣晨頓首頓首死罪

上傅大夫帝德所攝

顏母載靈大司農府君

司提橚司空

死罪臣盡心思

情所思惟臣

令宰長吏百姓

禋祀祠長吏百姓

籍備廟

靈遷速徙奉

日伏念孔子

德神聖所以

頴育賣臣晨長史

頓首恩霖伏

死寢寢守宅

頴寢臣晨長

周寍孝世無為

釋文：

相河南史君諱晨。字伯時。從越騎校尉拜。建寧元年四月十一日戊子到官。乃以令日拜謁孔

子。望見闕觀。式路虔跽。既至升堂。屏氣拜手。祗肅屑僾。髣髴若在。依依舊宅。神之所安。春秋復

禮。稽度玄靈。而無公出享獻之薦。欽因春饗。導物嘉會。述脩壁雍。社稷品制。即上尚書。參以符

驗。乃敢承祀。餘胙賦賜。刊石勒銘。并列本奏。大漢延期。彌歷億萬。

時長史廬江舒李謙敬讓。五官掾魯孔暢。功曹史孔淮。戶曹掾薛東門榮。史文陽馬琮。守廟百

石孔讚。副掾孔綱。故尚書孔立元世。河東大守孔彪元上。處土孔襃文禮。皆會廟堂。國縣員吏

律。八音克諧。蕩邪反正。奉爵稱壽。并畔官文學先生。執事諸弟子。合九百七人。雅歌吹笙。考之六

吏無大小。空府竭寺。咸僊來觀。于穆肅雍。上下蒙福。長享利貞。與天無極。

史君饗後。部史仇誧。縣吏劉耽等。補完里中道之周左廬垣壞決。作屋塗色。脩通大溝。西流

里外。南注城池。恐縣吏斂民。侵擾百姓。自以城池道濡麥給令還所斂民錢材。

史君念孔瀆顏母井去市遼遠。百姓酤買。不能得香酒美肉。於昌平亭下立會市。因彼左右。

咸所願樂。

又勅。瀆井。復民餝治。桐車馬於瀆上。東行道。表南北。各種一行梓。

假夫子冢顏母开舍及魯公冢守吏凡四人。月與佐除。

（唐人題名）大周天授二年（西元六九一年）二月廿三日。金台

觀主馬元貞。弟子楊景初。郭希玄

奉勅於東岳作功德。便謁

孔夫子之廟。題石記之。內品官楊君尚。歐陽智琮。宣德郎行兗州都督府倉曹參軍事李叔度。

魏 黃初元年魯孔子廟之碑

〈魯孔子廟之碑〉又稱〈孔羨碑〉，今存曲阜孔廟。三國魏黃初元年（二二〇）刻，記孔子二十一世孫孔羨受封宗聖侯，併奉孔子祀、修孔廟事。字體承自漢隸，書風遒勁寒儉，茂密雄強，結體嚴謹，骨力健勁，氣勢瑰偉，用筆方齊質拙，如斬釘截鐵，開六朝分楷先河，為魏隸代表，昔人評為魏刻之冠。

孔子嫡系後裔世襲受封，始於漢高祖封孔子九世孫孔騰為「奉祀君」。兩漢封號以褒成侯為主，至魏改號宗聖侯。沿用最久的封號是北宋所封「衍聖公」，直至民國二十四年（一九三五），南京國民政府府改孔子七十七代孫孔德成（一九二〇－二〇〇八）為「奉祀官」為止。

釋文：

魯孔子廟之碑。

維黃初元年。大魏受命。胤軒轅之高緃。紹虞氏之遺統。應歷數以改物。揚仁風以作教。於是揖五瑞。斑宗

彝。鈞衡石。同度量。秩群祀於無文。順天時以布化。既乃緝熙聖緒。昭顯上世。追存二代三恪之禮。秉紹宣

尼園成之後。以魯縣百戶。命孔子廿一世孫議郎孔羨為宗聖侯。以奉孔子之祀。

制詔三公曰。昔仲尼姿大聖之才。懷帝王之器。當衰周之末。而無受命之運。生平魯衛之朝。教化乎洙

泗之上。栖栖焉。皇皇焉。欲屈己以存道。貶身以救世。當時王公終莫能用。乃追考五代之禮。脩園王之事。

因魯史而制春秋。就大師而正雅頌。俾千載之後。莫不采其文以述作。仰其聖以成謀。咨可謂命世大聖。

億載之師表者。已遭天下大亂。百祀墮壞。舊居之廟毀而不脩。褒成之後絕而莫繼。闕里不聞講誦之聲。

四時不睹烝嘗之位。斯豈所謂崇化報功。盛德百世必祀者哉。嗟乎。朕是閔焉。其以議郎孔羨為宗聖侯。

邑百戶。奉孔子之祀。令魯邵脩起舊廟。置百石吏卒以守衛之。又於其外廣為屋宇。以居學者。於是魯之

父老。諸生遊士。睹廟堂之始復。觀俎豆之初設。嘉聖靈於髣髴。想貞祥之來集。乃慨然而歎曰。大道衰廢。

禮學滅絕卅餘年。

皇上懷仁聖之懿德。兼二儀之化育。廣大苞於無方。口恩淪於不測。故自受命以來。天人咸和。神氣烟熅。

嘉瑞踵武。休徵屢臻。殊俗解編髮而慕義。退夷越險阻而來賓。雖大皓遊龍以君世。虞氏儀鳳以臨民。佪

禹命玄宮而為夏后。西伯由岐社而為周文。尚何足稱於大魏哉。若乃紹繼微絕。興脩廢官。疇咨稽古。崇

配乾坤。允神明之所福祚。宇內之所歡也。豈徒魯邦而已哉。爾乃感殷人路寢之義。嘉先民泮宮之事。

以為高宗僖公。蓋嗣世之王。諸侯之國耳。猶著德於名頌。騰聲乎千載。況今

聖皇肇造。區夏創業。重統受命之曰。曾未下輿而褒崇。大聖隆化如此。能無頌乎。乃作頌曰。

煌煌大魏。受命溥將。苞體黃虞。含夏苞商。降釐下土。上清三光。群祀咸秩。靡事不綱。嘉彼玄聖。有邈其靈。

遭世霧亂。莫顯其榮。褎成旣絕。寢廟斯傾。闕里蕭條。靡歆靡馨。我皇悼之。尋其世武。乃建宗聖。以紹厥後。

脩復舊堂。豐其寢宇。莘莘學徒。爰居爰處。王教既備。群小遄沮。魯道以興。永作憲矩。洪聲登假。神祇來和。

休徵雜遝。瑞我邦家。內光區域。外被荒遐。殊方重譯。搏拊揚歌。於赫四聖。運世應期。仲尼既沒。文亦在茲。

彬彬我后。越而五之。並于億載。如山之基。

魏 李仲璇修孔子廟碑

28

〈李仲璇碑〉，全稱〈李仲璇修孔子廟碑〉，東魏興和三年（五四一）刻，現存曲阜孔廟。碑額以末端如爪之篆，書「魯孔子廟之碑」。文記兗州刺史李珽修繕孔廟頹牆，復塑孔子容像，且為孔門十賢立像事。碑文楷書，隸意為多，間雜有大小篆及分隸等書體，並大量使用異體字，反應當時流行的書藝風尚。

此碑為目前已知最早為孔子及十弟子塑像之紀錄。古時孔廟原有孔子塑像，明太祖（一三六八～一三九八）時因某些雕像無法表現孔子神態，下令爾後新蓋孔廟，皆以牌位取代塑像，明世宗嘉靖年間（一五二二～一五六六），命撤全國孔像，全以牌位祭祀，是為今日孔廟少見孔子塑像的原因。

處鳳皋雲弟虛斯女

優也峻之奇政績緝熙

鄩當像孔決日白言我

建綸密文譜是則從聖

紛密於像當未孔子日白於孔之陳廟察

亦青於文譜是則聖我人於孔之陳道察

人人白則道隱雖逝者如之美雨歟

業是以覲者莫斯逝莫義以斯之美時眇

怵惏焉

釋文：

魯孔子廟之碑。

粵若稽古。叡后欽明。文思衡宰。邁德丕顯。九功咸事。故能庸勳親賢。官方式敘。惟大魏徙鄴之五載。皇□興和之元年天□

咨寅賓出。曰。寔唯濟岱。宣風敷化。義屬英良。以君理思優敏。收民物望。斯允必能絃歌鄒魯。剋□□□□制□□□拜

我郡公使持節都督克州諸軍事車騎大將軍當州大都督克州刺史君。姓李字仲璇。趙國柏仁人也。其先帝高陽之苗裔。柱史之胤。

左車之綿緒。瑤光休彩。赫奕於上齡。若水嘉祥。扶踈于季葉。君以資解褐奉朝請。俄除定州平北府法曹參軍。仍曆□□功曹。諮議參

軍事。定相離三州長史。東郡汲郡恒農三郡太守。司徒左長史。中散太中大夫。營構都將。離克二州刺史。所在恩□。遺訓在民。夫椒桂

易地。而貞馥不移。君鳳舉雲翔。風期如一。妙與神同。恫然不樂。思仁未深。刑平惠和。□為淳□□階資寵□之榮。奕

葉重光之貴。氣韻優峻之奇。政績緝熙之美。既備於史傳與清頌。故不復詳載焉。君神懷踈爽。風度絕人。學業與□源並深。趣操共寒

松俱秀。故其隸克部也。嘗未浹旬。言觀孔廟。肅恭致誠。敬神如在。遂軔車曲埠。飲馬沂流。周遊眺覽。尚想伊人。□□慨然。有報功□□

之意。乃命工人。修建容像。孔子曰。從我于陳蔡者。皆不得及門也。因歷敘其才。以為四科之目。生既見從。沒□□侍。□□□。故顏氏□□□

奉進儒冠。于諸徒亦青衿青領。人亡則道隱。雖逝者如斯。風霜驟謝。而淪姿舊訊。曖似還新。至如廟宇凝靜。靈姿嚴麗。數仞之牆無以逾。七□之房

不能出。夫道系於人。是以睹之者莫不忻忻焉有入室登堂之想。斯亦化□之一隅也。今聖容肅穆。二五成行。丹素陸離。□□□似微笑而時言。

左右若承顏而受業。人亡則道隱。斯大義以之而乖。微言以之而絕。□□□。天誕聖哲。作民師□。風□闕里播□□洙泗。

至於歎鳳鳥之寂寥。傷河圖之莫出。屢應聘而不遇。知道德之不行。乃正雅頌。修春秋。刊理六經。懸諸日月。□□載之□□。

以述作。服其訓以成身。諂可謂開闢之儒聖。無窮之文宗者矣。此地古號曲埠。是唯魯都。雖宮觀荒毀。臺池□□。然其廟庭也。蔚質林

於九冬。罩修柯於百刃。類神栝之侵漢。同梧宮之巨圍。至夫鴻隨秋下。則月秀霜枝。燕逐春來。亦風開翠葉。既□□觀。□亦足以安

樂聖靈。是以無代不加修繕。庶億載以寧神。視民如傷。君清明在躬。精思入微。功被人神。德貫幽顯。豈惟營餝宣質經創□□□如虔修

岱像。崇奉玄宗。敦素羈華。與存廢絕。納之仁壽。體亡懷以幽詣。任萬物以為心。豈直靈津孤灑。虛光獨散者哉。夫一月之明。

可影百川。一人之鑒。從橫萬趣。爰自刺舉。未或斯同。然丹青所以圖盛□。金石所以刊不朽。□□不鐫。瑤瑤焉述。府州佐□□□□令

士民等。略序義目。樹碑廟庭。俾後來君子。知功業之若斯焉。乃作頌曰。

二儀肇泮。人倫攸舉。邈邈玄王。誕茲聖緒。祖習堯舜。獻章文武。聲溢九天。化潭八宇。祖習□□。聖神盡妙。化潭伊何。□□存教。□同麗

景。樑天孤昭。無異岱宗。巖巖特峭。重山隱寶。深霞秘暉。在哀之葉。自衛言歸。德生於予。文寶在茲。彝倫禮樂。剋敘書詩。□□驚異。灰管

流氣。良木其摧。緬踰千祀。以存恕亡。允諸靈意。不有伊人。熟云修置。唯君體道。布政優優。白鳩巢室。赤雀西樓。仁罔不備。智□□周。器

冠後哲。風邁前修。既繕孔像。復立十賢。誠兼岱宇。勤盡重玄。仰聖儀之煥爛。嘉鴻業之嬋聯。長無絕兮終古。永萬億兮斯傳。

興和三年十二月十一日訖功。

唐 裴孝智撰文宣王廟門記

29

又名〈文宣王廟新修三門記〉、〈文宣王廟新三門記〉，或〈新修文宣王廟門記〉，碑現在曲阜孔廟。記載大曆八年（七七三）兗州刺史孟休鑒、曲阜縣令裴有象新建曲阜孔廟廟門事蹟。由祠部員外郎兼侍御史裴孝智撰文，裴平書丹並篆額。碑文隸書，結字規整嚴謹，筆法秀俊，波拂勁挺，筆畫粗細反差較大，顯現中唐楷法入隸書風。

孔子身後歷代帝王為彰顯尊崇，不斷追封追諡。其中以唐代對孔子的封號變化最多：唐太宗尊其為「宣父」，高宗追贈為「太師」，武則天追封「隆道公」，唐玄宗開元二十七年（七三九），追諡孔子為文宣王，是孔子封王之始。

88

酉炎元耕歌扇　　　　　
秆火肵生之德漢
惟非讀血光沫淳
與官奄皇勸洽
祠曹中聖夫殷濃
廟之之人子周不
祿燭祿之聖故夢
　春熙鄉春典
福桼闢也與床楚
禧起里先名從德

釋文：

文宣王廟門記。

文宣王廟新門記。

朝散大夫檢校祠部外郎兼侍御史大夫裴孝智撰。

前義王府倉曹參軍裴平下丹并篆額。

成域中之大。歸天下之往曰王。二者應曆以宰物。酌時以觀化。威聲雷霆。不嚴

理合自然之運。不行家至契如神之速。德叶恊於幽明。道徜徉於古。始無爲無事。其大矣哉。

洎乎澆淳既變。仁義斯起。傴息庠序。棲遲洙泗。憲章萬物之首。馳騁百王之末。清潁波於幽

屬。扇儒術於殷周。故春秋作而賊亂懼。風興刪而廉恥生。美韶護而沾濡之音息。行揖讓而累

莊敬之心勸。夫子聖者歟。名與日月周流。業與乾坤終始。隱焉而光。闇然而彰。命服袞裳。巍如

代稱王。曲阜聖人之鄉也。先是閟宮霞敞。正殿岑立。繚以環堵。邃其臺門。巍若化造。嶷如□

動允所謂。淹中之勝蒦。闕里之全模。刺史孟公休鑒德潤。尊師道肥。希聖研精。百氏□□

言夜火非官曹之燭。春桑絕附校之詠。判官郡功曹盧瞳。以文發身。以清撿物。博通□□

數四科。惟此祠廟。厥初層搆。朱戶半傾。雕甍中落。難名之閫奧。造次可遊。如在之□□

易覩。將何以克恭過位。加敬及庭。於是孟公首之。盧公翊之。因命縣大夫兼大□□□

裴公新其南門。書時也。公名有象。廣學攻文。始登甲科。吏干舒二人□□□

等。吏于充二人悦服。蓄可大之用。爲致遠之資。由是庀葅程具乃役。不斬仲□□□

山之石。償以日。而給功不時而就。大屋橫亘。雙扉洞開。丹拱繡栭。膠葛固□□□

景飛檐騈。逼而棲霧。扃鐍既固。享獻聿修。官吏唯肅清之謹。邑人無□濆□□□

席及階而升數仞之牆。由戶而入。君子以非孟公之化不行。非盧公之□□□□

不成三事叶同□底于善孝智不敏儒家之流。徒挹春秋舍菜之禮。□□□□□

誌不腆之文。俾刊永貞之石。時大曆八年十二月一日也。

文宣王
廟門記
文宣王廟新門記
朝散大夫撿校祠部員外郎兼侍御史裴孝智撰

宋 建隆三年重修文宣王廟記

30

此碑現存西安碑林。北宋太祖建隆三年（九六二），
王彥超（九一四～九八六）立。內容敘述唐末昭宣帝天祐
元年（九○四）將長安舊城「太學并石經」遷至新城內事，
是已知最早記載唐代石經遷置經過之碑。碑文行書為典型
北宋宮廷書風，碑額「玄聖文宣王」為真宗大中祥符元年
（一○○八）加諡後刻。立碑人王彥超，字德升，《宋史》
有傳，五代至北宋初年著名將領，封邠國公，贈尚書令。
除刻此碑外，亦曾摹刻數度火毀的唐虞世南〈孔子廟堂
碑〉。

傳承長安國子學四書五經的西安碑林，和曲阜孔廟，
這兩處中國規模最大碑林皆與孔子有關。

連從□文竇王廟記
昔莊先王法龜圖而
知天地之變道考注知
知而揩矣北親□則
投濟國有庠鄉有投
仲尼之道揭而行之

釋文：

玄聖文宣王廟大門記。

重修文宣王廟記。觀察判官朝散大夫撿校尚書工部貟外郎兼殿中侍御史劉從[乂]撰（上缺）[馬]昭吉書并篆額。

昔在先王。法龜圖而畫卦。降于中古。效鳥蹟而成文。吉凶生而爻象興。仁義[起]（下缺）所以察鬼神之情狀。窮

天地之變通。考往知來。鈎深索隱。則物無遁形矣。是知典墳者。所以復父子之[孝]慈。正君[口口]法。立言垂範。與士作程。則人

知所措矣。非規[矩]則不能定方圓之用。非準繩則不能質曲直之疑。憲章開八政之源。名教挈五常之器。必由是也。何其盛[口]。

故得國有庠。鄉有校。黨有序。家有塾。雖設教不倫。其歸一揆。譬乎貞筠勁挺。假[箬]羽以滋深。美璞琭奇成。琮[瓗]而益貴。然後[口]

仲尼之道。揭而行之。与日月以俱懸。仲尼之德。推而廣之。與江河[而]同潤。輔相

皇王之大業。天縱多能。弥綸宇宙之全功。日彰聖績。其於遺風餘烈。賈古輝[今]。[口口]復書。昔唐之季也。大盜尋戈。權臣竊命。地

維絕紐。八鑾遷脅於東周。天邑成墟。三輔悉奔於南雍。天祐甲子歲。太尉許國[口][公]時為居守。繾務葺修。遂移太學并石經於

此。露往霜來。彤墻半圮。塵封蘇駁。塑像全隳。屬吾道之有歸。見斯文之不墜。

我太師令公稟嶽秀川靈之英綮。負虎眉犀額之雄標。張智勇以經邦。立誠明而馭下。鳴鍾沸鼓。辛勤

討伐之勳。攬轡登車。慷慨澄清之志。

皇帝闡統之明年也。念漢五陵之豪族。桀驁輕浮。秦四塞之要衝。推埋剽掠。將[祛][故]態。每念難材。閫外牙璋。方思宿將關中。管

鑰荐。委通賢。一角來而上應玉繩。九苞鳴而動諧金奏。仰分憂[寄]。旁奉政條。投惠而民懷。發奸而吏懍。申明獄

訟。引決如神。勸課耕來。服勤務本。令出而隨如注塋。化行而速若置郵。加以鈐閣曉開。劇談名理。玳筵夜合。高會英儒。一日因

謁靈祠。顧謂賓佐曰。厚祿高官。咸稱弟子。隳垣壞宇。孰念宗師。豈[口口]務通方。不資於國耶。致功成利無益於民

耶。觀風吏斂袵而對曰。昔者仲尼生於周之末世。事於魯之亂邦。長幼失宜。冠婚亡序。繇是刪詩書而定禮樂。贊易

象而修春秋。扶世導民。勞形役智。卑棲下位。則席不暇溫。歷聘諸矦。則車無停響。斥于齊而逐于宋。厄于衛而困于陳。每屈己

以救時。欲化風而成俗。昭王厚禮。固輕千社之封矧寸祿乎。靈公奇待。不顧万鍾之[粟]。矧束脩乎。孟軻所謂生人已來。未有如

夫子者也。功如是。德如是。豈無益於民乎。豈無資於國乎。

我太師令公取製度之規。以模黌舍量經營之費。遂出俸財。霞張夢奠之楹。粉耀藏書之壁。增華崇麗。眩目驚心。青璅丹梁。

宣聖文
宣王廟
大門記

見廊廡軒墀之潔。漢扃蕭帳有豆籩庋櫝之儀。莫不賦采揮毫。糸靈運思。堯身禹狀。□神凛凛以如生月。角山庭畫像莘莘

而在列。介珪華袞。享王爵於高封。八簋三牲。遵國章於常祀。工徒告畢。廟貌斯嚴。英旄□□之賢瞻之如市。挹讓周旋之教。靡

若從風。里閭焜耀於搢紳。文雅闡揚於洙泗。從義廟摘蘗。才類編苦。叙美圖芳。俾刊貞琰。□課拙強扣庸音。時大宋建隆三

年八月二十五日記。

推誠奉義翊戴功臣永興軍節度管內觀察處置等使特進撿校太師兼中書令行京兆尹上柱國琅琊郡開國公食邑四千五□□戶食實封一千三百戶王。彥超。安

仁祚刻字。

三 歷代尊儒

　　孔子也許是對中國產生最大影響的人，其影響力見於歷史長流當中，如荀、孟諸子之言、歷代叢出的解經衍繹之書、名儒秉持孔子精神所撰寫的箴言、以及清代大量被翻譯成滿語的四書五經之中。此外，各地孔廟的御賜匾額，也能看出孔子歿世而名稱，受到歷代帝王追尊的無比殊榮。

清 聖祖 御筆書萬世師表

清聖祖愛新覺羅‧玄燁（一六五四－
一七二二），崇尚儒學、理學，平生勤
於書藝，曾臨晉唐以來古帖，後得沈荃
（一六二四－一六八四）指點，習董其昌
（一五五五－一六三六）行書並兼取宋元
名家。

孔子第六十七代嫡長孫孔毓圻
（一六五七－一七二三）《幸魯盛典》
載，康熙二十三年歲次甲子（一六八四）
聖祖駕幸孔子故居，頒贈御書「萬世師
表」卷；並於次年下詔摹揚此匾頒贈天下
文廟」。

本幅原為孔府文物，字體敦厚，下
筆沉穩，力道勻稱，收筆峻快果決，是罕
見的聖祖御筆擘窠大字佳作。字畫層次清
晰，筆蹤毫芒靡遺，信是目前各地孔廟聖
祖御筆賜匾所祖原蹟。

98

師表

康熙甲子孟冬敬書

99

清 沈荃 書伊川四箴

沈荃（一六二四－一六八四），江蘇華亭（今上海）人。字貞蕤，號繹堂，別號充齋。順治進士，官至禮部侍郎，工詩善書，學行醇潔。此四箴是世稱「伊川先生」的宋代理學大師程頤（一〇三二－一一〇七），據《論語・顏淵》中，顏淵問仁，孔子答以「克己復禮」，「非禮勿視，非禮勿听，非禮勿言，非禮勿動」發展而成的道德戒律。

沈荃書法初學董其昌（一五五五－一六三六），晚歲得力於米芾（一〇五二－一一〇八）甚深。曾於康熙朝奉召入宮，與皇帝談論古今書法。書風充分反映出「康雍之世，專仿香光」現象。此為沈氏五十四歲之作，敧側秀雅，結字氣韻深受董其昌影響。

釋文：

視箴曰。心兮本虛。應物無迹。操之有要。蔽交於前。其中則遷。制之於外。以
安其內。克己復禮。久而誠矣。聽箴曰。人有秉彝。本乎天性。知誘物化。遂亡其正。卓
彼先覺。知止有定。閑邪存誠。非禮勿聽。言箴曰。人心之動。因言以宣。發禁躁妄。內
斯靜專。矧是樞機。興戎出好。吉凶榮辱。惟其所召。傷易則誕。傷煩則支。己肆物忤。出
悖來違。非法不道。欽哉訓辭。動箴曰。哲人知幾。誠之於思。志士厲行。守之於為。順
理則裕。從欲惟危。造次克念。戰兢自持。習與性成。聖賢同歸。

右錄伊川四箴。康熙丁巳（西元一六七七年）六月。日講官起居注詹事府詹事兼翰林院侍讀學士臣沈荃。

清 張照 書御製讀大學衍義詩

張照（一六九一－一七四五），華亭（今上海松江）人，字得天，號涇南，又號天瓶居士。康熙四十八年（一七〇九）進士，官至刑部尚書，諡文敏。通釋典，研法律，精音樂，尤工書法。初從董其昌（一五五一－一六三六），繼乃出入米芾（一〇五一－一一〇八）、顏真卿（七〇九－七八五），天骨開張，氣魄渾厚，雄跨當代，深被宸賞。

《大學衍義》作者真德秀（一一七八－一二三五），南宋著名理學家，秉承朱子學術思想，書中治國之道和廉政文化為後世推崇，康熙皇帝稱為「力明正學」，是盛清皇族必讀書之一。

本幅書清高宗乾隆皇帝（一七一一－一七九九）御製詩，結字縝密，佈置停勻。書體若楷若行，頗有顏朱風韻。

釋文：

晴牕披典墳。望古興邈想。睠惟
希元翁。體道粹涵養。著有衍義
書。妙蘊資尋倣。大含亦細入。渟
泓包萬象。孔曾緒不墜。千載揭
昭朗。讀書思其人。高山欣景仰。
御製讀大學衍義詩。臣張照敬書。

晴牕披典墳望古興邈想睠惟

希元翁體道粹涵養著有衍義

書妙蘊資尋倣大含亦細入渟

泓包萬象孔曾緒不墜千載揭

昭朗讀書思其人高山欣景仰

御製讀大學衍義詩　臣張照敬書

清 楊峴 隸書焦氏易林

34

楊峴（一八一九－一八九六），字見山，號藐翁、遲鴻殘叟，歸安（今浙江）人。咸豐五年（一八五五）舉人，官常州知府。工詩文，善書法，八分書可謂繼往開來。《焦氏易林》作者焦延壽，字贛，一說名贛，字延壽。西漢梁國（治在今河南商丘南）人，此書體裁大抵四字一句，內容闡釋易學要義。據說現今卜筮所常用「京房易」的作者京房是其弟子。

此軸作於光緒十一年（一八九一），楊峴七十三歲。書法風格源自〈禮器碑〉，但用筆提按和用墨濕涸變化，以及結字之開闔舒展處皆能自創新境，氣勢懾人心神，獨樹一幟。

以漢隸節錄書之，適得其所。

釋文：

新田宜粟。上農得穀。可以
服食。保全家國。神鳥五色。
鳳皇為主。集於王國。使君
得所。福喜入門。與君相索。
使我有得。光緒辛卯（西元一八九一年）十月。
七十三歲孱叟楊峴。

清 康有為 書孟子

35

康有為（一八五八－一九二七），原名祖詒，字廣廈，號長素、更生。廣東南海人。光緒二十四年（一八九八）推行「戊戌變法」而未成，史稱「百日維新」。作書取法〈石門頌〉，著《廣藝舟雙楫》，抑帖揚碑。本幅為黃莉容、黃文如女士捐贈，書《孟子》〈盡心〉之一章：「萬物皆備于我矣。反身而誠，樂莫大矣。強恕而行，求仁莫近焉。」

概言萬物之理皆具於己身，求仁之道，在誠與恕，反省自身，推己及人。此作行筆流暢，用筆遲澀，結字緊結而向外舒展，開張峻拔，筆力雄健。整體氣勢弘張，而不究點畫，乃康氏書風特色。

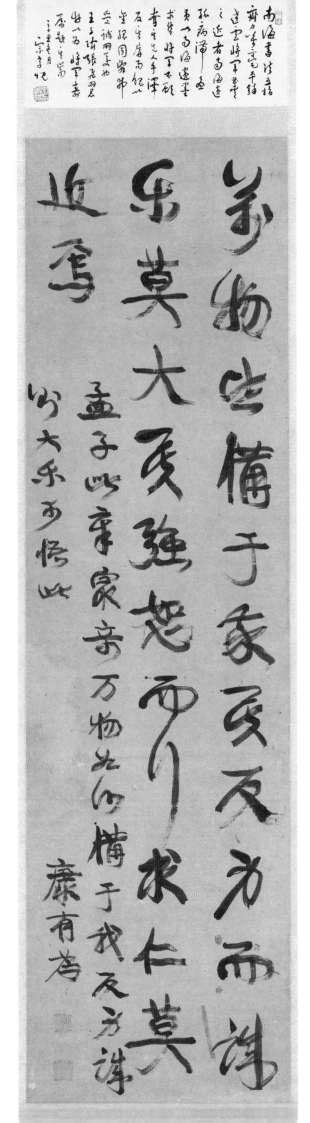

釋文：

萬物皆備于我矣。反身而誠。

樂莫大矣。強恕而行。求仁莫

近焉。孟子此章最奇。萬物如何備于我。反身誠

則大樂。可悟此。康有為。

民國 沈曾植 草書孔子家語

沈曾植（一八五二—一九二二），字子培，號巽齋，一號乙龕，晚號寐叟，別署乙公，浙江嘉興人。光緒六年（一八八○）進士，官安徽布政使。學識淹博，書法早年精於帖學，後融漢隸、北碑、章草為一爐，自成面目。兼作山水小幅，淡雅有韻致。

本幅以行草書節錄記載孔子與弟子言行、事蹟的《孔子家語》二則，分別為〈觀周第十一〉與〈顏回第十八〉，旨在闡明言語貴精不在多的重要性。全作參以〈爨寶子碑〉法，強調用筆變化，抑揚盡致，委曲得宜，體勢飛揚險峻，姿態沉實樸茂，奇趣橫出，翻覆盤旋。具有強烈個性與風格，推測為晚年之作。

釋文：

孔子觀周。遂入太祖后稷之廟。廟右階之前。有金人焉。參緘其口。而銘其背曰。古之慎言人也。戒之哉。無多言。多言多敗。無多事。多事多壞。安樂必戒。言以何悔。仲孫問於顏子曰。一言而有益於智。智乎。曰。一言而有益於智。預也。一言而有益於仁。恕也。吟江仁兄屬書格言。為錄家語二則。寐叟。

孔子聞之入太祖之殿東望之
見人不在參殿下而誚者曰古之帳
之人也戒之哉勿之多言多言多敗
事之多墙必戒之哉無多事多
孫此於額子曰一言而可以濟於智
言以於智預也一言而可以廢於知也

哈江仁兄屬書
龍之多綠宗達
公 寅生

民國 溥儒 滿文書大學

溥儒（一八九六－一九六三），字心畬，號西山逸士，恭親王奕訢之孫，清室貴冑，世居北京。幼即究心詩詞、經史、書畫。潛心丹青，以臨摹古書畫入手，與張大千並稱「南張北溥」。後遷居來臺，為臺灣近代最重要的國畫大家之一。

本幅為寒玉堂寄存，以滿文官書體錄《大學》，起自「大學之道」，止於「未之有也」。款題：「以上經一章，溥儒。」清代統治者秉持「道統即治統」原則，重視儒家經典，作為合理統治中國的理論依據。康熙年間（一六六二－一七二二）即譯四書成滿文，成為經筵日講的材料。儒家修身、齊家、治國、平天下的理念，也影響了滿族思想文化。

後附參考圖版為清代乾隆年間（一七三六－一七九五）《御製繙譯四書》滿漢文對照本《大學》，及滿語羅馬拼音轉寫與其詞意注釋。

大甲曰
顧諟天之明命

康誥曰
克明德

而門人記之也

之

右經一章
蓋孔子之言而曾子述
則曾子之意

而其所薄者厚未之有也

其本亂而末治者否矣
其所厚者薄

庶人
壹是皆以脩身為本

而后天下平
自天子以至於

家齊而后國治
國治

意誠而后心正
心正而

后身脩
身脩而后家齊

知至
知至而后意誠

致知在格物
物格而后

欲誠其意者　先致其知

欲正其心者　先誠其意

欲脩其身者　先正其心

欲齊其家者　先脩其身

先治其國　欲治其國者　先齊其家

古之欲明明德於天下者

知所先後　則近道矣

得

物有本末　事有終始

知止而后有定

安而后能慮　慮而后能

靜而后能安　定而后能靜

大學之道

在親民　在明明德

在止於至善

則庶乎其不差矣

13　gūnin be　unenggi obuki serengge, neneme sarasu de isibumbi.
　　意　把　誠　欲成為　者，　　先　知識　在　使致。

14　sarasu de　isiburengge, jaka be hafure de bi. jaka be
　　知　於　使致者，　物　把　通曉　在。　物　把

15　hafuka manggi, sarasu isinambi. sarasu isinaha manggi, gūnin unenggi
　　格　　後，　知　　致。　知　致了　後，　意　誠

16　ombi. gūnin unenggi oho manggi, mujilen tob ombi. mujilen
　　可。意　誠　了　後，　心　正可。　心

17　tob oho manggi, beye tuwancihiyabumbi. beye tuwancihiyabuha manggi,
　　正了　後，　身　　修。　身　　使修了　　後，

18　boo teksilebumbi. boo teksilebuhe manggi, gurun dasabumbi. gurun
　　家　使齊。　家　使齊了　後，　國　治，　國

19　dasabuha manggi, abkai fejergi necin ombi. abkai jui ci,　geren
　　使治了　後，　天的　下　平　可。　天的　子自，　庶眾

20　niyalma de isitala, bireme gemu beyebe tuwancihiyara be da obuhabi.
　　人　於直到，　一概　都　把身　　修的　　為　本　使成為。

21　da facuhūn oci, dube dasaburengge akū. jiramin ningge be
　　本　紊亂　若，　末　使治者　沒有。　厚　者　把

22　nekeliyeleneci, nekeliyen ningge, jiramilanjire kooli　akū.
　　若弄薄了，　　薄　者，　　弄厚了　舊例　沒有。

23　dergi nomun i emu fiyelen.　　　　　pu žu
　　上　經　的一　章　　　　　　　　溥儒

1　amba tacin i doro, genggiyen erdemu be genggiyelere de bi,
　　大　學　的 道，　明　　　德　把　明白的　　　在，

2　irgen be icemlere de bi. ten i sain de ilinara de bi.
　　民 把 革新的　在。極致 的　善 於　止的　在。

3　ilinara be saha manggi teni tokton ombi. tokton oho manggi,
　　止的 把 知道了 後　才　定的 是。　定　了　後，

4　teni cibsen ome mutembi. cibsen oho manggi, teni elhe ome
　　才　靜的　為　能　靜的　了　後，才　安　為

5　mutembi. elhe oho manggi teni seoleme mutembi. seolehe manggi,
　　能　安　了　以後　才　思慮　　能。思慮　以後，

6　teni bahame mutembi. jaka de da dube bi. baita de tuhen,
　　才　得到　能　物 於 本 末 有。事 於 終結，

7　deribun bi. nenden amaga be saha de, doro de hanci oho kai.
　　始　有。先　　後　把 知道了 時，道 於 近 了 矣。

8　julgei genggiyen erdemu be abkai fejergi de genggiyeleki serengge,
　　昔日的　明　　　德 把 天的 下 於 欲明　　者，

9　neneme gurun be dasambi. gurun be dasaki serengge, neneme boo be
　　先　國 把 治理。國 把 欲治　者，　先　家 把

10　teksilembi. boo be teksileki serengge, neneme beyebe tuwancihiyambi,
　　整齊。家 把 欲齊　者，先 把身　　端正，

11　beyebe tuwancihiyaki serengge, neneme mujilen be tob obumbi.
　　把身　欲端正　　者，先　心 把 正 使成為

12　mujilen be tob obuki serengge, neneme gūnin be unenggi obumbi.
　　心 把 正 欲成為 者，先　意 把 誠 使成為。

漢高帝

清 沈振麟 繪帝鑑圖說

明神宗朱翊鈞（一五六三—一六二〇）十歲繼位，輔臣張居正（一五二五—一五八二）等取歷代帝王事一百一十七則，每則故事配圖繪一幅，編成《帝鑑圖說》，以為培育賢君之教材。

此清內府圖繪寫本。畫家沈振麟（西元十九世紀），字鳳池，吳縣人（今江蘇蘇州），咸豐、同治年間（一八五一—一八七四）供奉內廷，擅長人物寫照，畫名甚高。本幅〈過魯祀聖〉繪漢高祖十二年（前一九五）平英布之亂返京，途經曲阜，以最高規格的祭品，牛、羊、豬太牢三牲祭孔，並封孔子九代孫孔騰為「奉祀君」，專主孔子祀事。此例遂成為後世天子祭孔典範。

漢史紀高帝擊淮南王黥布還過

魯以太牢祀孔子

解西漢史上記漢高帝因淮南
王黥布謀反自領兵征之擒了
黥布得勝回還經過山東曲阜
縣乃舊魯國是孔子所生的地
方有孔子的墳墓高帝具太牢
牲禮親拜祭之 叫祭祀太的牛夫孔
子雖是大聖其官不過魯國的
大夫自孔子歿後戰國之君皆
不知尊信其道及秦始皇又焚
燒其書高帝以天子之尊方用
兵征伐之際就知崇儒重道且
用太牢與社稷宗廟的祭禮一
樣後世人君尊敬孔子實自高
帝始其好尚正大如此宜其為
一代創業之君也

清 蔣元樞 重修臺郡各建築圖說

　蔣元樞（一七三八－一七八一），字仲升，號香巖，江蘇常熟人，詞臣畫家蔣廷錫（一六六九－一七三二）之孫，乾隆二十四年（一七五九）舉人，乾隆四十年（一七七五）至四十三年任臺灣知府，四十一至四十二年兼護理分巡臺灣道，任內多有建樹。本幅〈孔廟禮器圖〉選自《重修臺郡各建築圖說》，乾隆四十一年因「臺郡孔廟皆用鉛錫，已屬陋質，至豆、籩、簠、簋，既非合度，且多未備」，故「元樞謹按闕里制度，自吳中選匠設局，購銅鼓鑄備，造禮樂各器，計用銅萬餘，解運來臺」。翌年親撰碑記，與董事陳作霖（約活動於十八至十九世紀）、林朝英（一七三九－一八一六）勒石記事，碑現存於臺南孔廟，是早期臺灣尊孔的重要文獻。

香盒　　花瓶　　毛血盤　　罍　　抖

犧尊　　著尊　　勺　　帛篚
銅坫　　銅坫

燭其罩　　雷尊　　銅香盤　　瘞鍁

銅坫　　洗

茅沙池

四 經典圖繪

西漢以後，孔子思想日益受到帝王重視，政府大力推行的儒家倫理道德深入人心，調節維繫君臣、父子、兄弟、夫婦、朋友間的關係，並成為士人以天下國家為己任的精神指導，是社會安定的重要力量。孔子所崇敬的勇者卞莊子、採集的詩篇等，甚至孔門弟子的故事等，都被畫成配合文本相互參照的圖繪。

40

宋人 卞莊子刺虎圖

卞莊子是魯國（前一〇二七─前二五〇）卞邑大夫，有一舉而獲二虎之勇，齊人懼之，不敢伐魯。此卷所畫故事，見於《戰國策》及《史記・張儀列傳》，故事意涵與鷸蚌相爭類似。畫中一牛已倒斃於草上，二虎爭牛而鬥。卞莊子持劍欲行刺虎。一人上前勸止，謂待虎鬥畢，再行刺虎則可以逸代勞。卷後負劍、奉軸、操杖、執如意者六人。本幅無款，筆法細勁，畫虎虎相鬥，卞莊子之勇，均為宋畫古風，極為生動。

《論語・憲問第十四》孔子答子路成人之問，即以卞莊子為勇者範例。子路與卞莊子同為卞邑之人，崇尚孝親武勇或為其地風俗。

傳元 王振鵬畫柯九思寫 豳風圖

豳，在岐山北，為周先世立國之地。據說成王（?—西元前一○二一）幼年繼位，周公（?—西元前一○三二）攝政，為令成王了解農桑為政教首務，並關心百姓的四季生活，作豳風曉諭周人祖先后稷、公劉稼穡重農的傳統。此卷圖繪〈豳風·七月〉，為孔子所輯《詩經》十五國風中最長的一首，由農事之始寫至農事之終，先寫衣食，次敘農耕蠶桑，最後論至打獵與秋收冬藏，共計八段，全卷青綠設色，每段旁書原文參照。舊題與跋均以為是元代王振鵬（活動於十四世紀前半），及柯九思（一二九○—一三四三）作品，然畫中已見明代仇英（約一四九四—一五五二）影響，推測應為十六世紀後蘇州畫家託名之作。

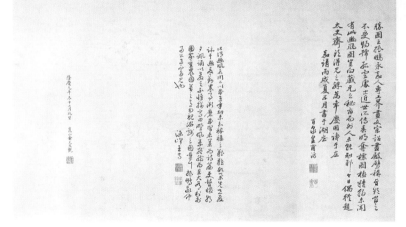

129

元 趙孟頫 甕牖圖

趙孟頫（一二五四－一三二二），字子昂，號松雪道人。詩文清遠，書畫復唐宋古風，為後世所宗。圖繪子貢見原憲於其居所，桑木為門軸，破甕為窗口之陋室，以昭示君子以德樂道之理，故事出於《史記・仲尼弟子列傳》。端木賜，字子貢，衛人。少孔子三十一歲，經商相魯致富。原憲，宋人，少孔子二十六歲，樂道隱居而貧。

本幅山石無皴，僅鉤勒輪廓，後填以青綠，人物衣紋行筆柔暢有力，有唐人古風。畫幅右下有千字文「索」字編號，卷後則有項元汴題識「明嘉靖卅年（一五五八）秋八月重裝于天籟閣」，並有「原價五十兩」之記述。

原憲（前五一五－？），字子思，又稱原思。魯人，早期入孔門的弟子之一。在孔子仕魯任司寇期間，擔任家邑宰，據說在孔子逝後即隱居不仕。《論語・憲問》記錄了原憲問恥、問仁，《論語・雍也》亦記其推辭任宰的九百斛俸米，後因孔子勸其可用於周濟鄰里而收受。《孔子家語》稱其「清靜守節，貧而樂道」，唐玄宗追封「原伯」，宋真宗加封「任城侯」。

明嘉靖卅年秋八月重裝于天籟閣
元趙松雪做趙千里刷色畫原憲甕牖圖逸品
明崇禎甲戌年夏重裱于樂志堂
墨林項元汴珍秘
原價五十兩
索

右子貢見原憲圖畫見貧
無詔富無驕之言乃為畫
其軼事耳故二子同出夫子
之門以道德為悅豈以貧富
為煒哉子昂

連騎擁蓋谷口通下車欽
進步廷佇觀書竊瞬眸
蓋者非痛誰貪意自形
庚寅仲春滿題

141

文　寧　王　新　門　記　朝　散　義　大

成　中　之　大　歸　天　下　之　望　曰　如　一　大

理　舍　白　然　足　運　不　家　斯　運　恩　如　三

追　扇　淺　淳　然　變　仁　義　斯　起　定　奕　賊　庠　神

漢　儒　林　於　熟　憂　故　春　起　運　契　前　王　二

壯　欲　之　勸　殷　周　聖　者　麻　奠　息　義　大

文　舜　王　色　皇　聖　夫　子　重　之　郎　光　閣

言　　敷　　裴　　寺　　立　　章　　席
龍　　四　　夫　　之　　六　　泉　　父
新　　　　亏　　帝　　楣　　階
其　　　　克　　　　宜　　驛　　宋
門　　心　　　　口　　　　遠　　外
書　　恢　　　　亦　　棲　　示　　敷
服　　時　　給　　　　霧　　　　尺
奮　　也　　功　　　　局　　　　藩
可　　大　　　　既　　　　由　　戶

繪畫中的孔子形象與書法裡的儒家主題

吳誦芬

摘要

中國歷史上，從沒有另一個能和孔子造成相同影響的人。

即使經過數千年，不僅孔子的思想，至今依舊是華人世界權衡輕重的價值標竿；孔子本人的身影，和歷代政權對他追尊的餘緒仍處處可見。除了四書五經、史籍故事，在古代被用以成教化、助人倫的繪畫，以及為昭功烈，以傳後世的刻石中，孔子相關議題也極受重視，並常因此而被妥善保存。

今日我們可在書畫文物當中見到的孔子相關主題，最為有趣的大概有：一、一人多貌─傳說中的孔子到底長得甚麼樣？

二、周邊文存─要在文人之祖孔子門前現書法亮文章，可比班門弄斧。能拿得進孔廟的文章書法都經常是一時之選，更不用說是歷代帝王經常親自以御筆題字頒賜碑匾，用對孔子的尊重來彰顯自己是以延續聖人法統為己任的明主賢君。本文將聚焦於此兩大議題，介紹各種出於後世尊崇仰慕，時而不時出現在各種書畫文物當中的孔子形貌與封賜遺蹟。

前言

孔子（西元前五五一～西元前四四九）是家喻戶曉的聖人，距今兩千多年以前，孔子開創了有教無類的私人講學之風，使得教育從貴族之學，普及到庶民百姓。千百年來，孔子的主張除了思想與學說教育的傳遞，其政治上德治化民、倫理仁政等口號，也被統治階級採納運用，作為安定天下的重要力量。孔子刪詩書，贊周易，訂禮樂，修春秋，他所編述的著作，成為歷代科舉取士的必讀教材，影響華夏文化至為深遠。此外，鄰近的日本、韓國、越南以及東南亞等地區，亦受其學說霑溉，形成了儒家文化圈。

孔子被孟子尊為「聖之時者」，意思是其思想能適用於各個時代。

今日，在大家紛紛崇尚國際化、現代化的同時，孔子的學行非但沒有被往事塵封，反而突破時空，益發煥爛的成為西方世界也樂於接受的潮流；在某些地方，孔子甚至還被賦予神性，成為學子們祈求考運的對象。

孔子時感嘆：「天不生仲尼，萬古如長夜。」孔子為華夏文明燃起的漢代著名史學家司馬遷（約西元前一四五－約前九〇），在論及曙光，代有才人薪火傳承，漸趨發揚。歷代宿學大儒為了解經而作傳，再為了推演傳義而作疏、箋、章句、正義、集解等等，民間甚至發展了依託經義，專論神學瑞應現象等的緯書。研究孔子生平、思想、學說的諸家著作早已浩瀚如海，孔子的言行、事蹟，與周遊列國的見聞，亦皆保存於《論語》、《孔子家語》，或散見於《史記》與諸子百家經史故事之中。

然而，不僅只是典籍文獻，中華傳統藝術其實也受到孔子思想浸漬霑溉，極具文人性質。本院所藏書法、繪畫、書籍版畫中與孔子相關視覺材料量數眾多，因此，筆者特意選取其中優質佳作，希望藉由此展，再次喚起社會大眾對於孔子的關注。

本文將分為繪畫（含版畫）與書法兩大部分，介紹孔子在傳統藝術中的身影姿態與影響力。有趣的是，與孔子相關的畫作常以孔子的生平事蹟為題材，而書法中所反映的則是歷代帝王、官員、仕紳與孔氏子孫對孔子源遠流長的尊崇敬慕。為使讀者由淺入深理解孔子其人其事和歷代的尊孔追封，以下將先介紹孔子家世生平與歷代進封追尊大事，再採先畫後書的順序，依次說明。

（一）孔子家世生平與歷代追尊概況

孔子，名丘，字仲尼，後世敬稱孔子或孔夫子。其祖輩可追溯到子姓的殷商王族。西周初年封紂王（約活動於西元前十二~十一世紀）的庶兄微子啟於宋國，其弟微仲八傳子孫的其中一位孔父嘉（約活動於西元前八世紀），以孔為氏，別為公族，成為孔家始祖。宋殤公十年（西元前七一〇），宋國太宰華父督弒君作亂，孔父嘉的曾孫防叔為了躲避滅門之禍而奔魯，孔子之父叔梁紇（？~西元前五四九）即為防叔之孫。（詳見孔子世系表）

叔梁紇曾為魯國郰邑大夫，履立戰功，先娶施氏，生九女無子，其妾生子孟皮，但因孟皮足疾不能主祭，故叔梁紇晚年求娶顏氏，禱於尼山，生孔子，取名為丘，字仲尼。[1]

孔子三歲喪父，十七歲喪母。十五歲志於學，謂已少賤，故多能鄙事。十九歲娶宋國并官氏為妻，翌年得子孔鯉。孔子一生的為官經歷，曾擔任魯國季孫氏管理倉廩的委吏、主管魯君苑囿畜牧事的乘田吏、地方官中都宰、掌水利營建等事的司空，以及魯國最高司法官員大司寇。（詳見孔子年表）

魯定公十年（西元前五〇〇年），孔子主持魯定公與齊景公夾谷之會，使齊歸還侵占魯的汶陽等地，取得外交上的勝利，是為孔子官職生涯的高峰。魯定公十三年（西元前五〇三年），孔子為重立魯國公室權威，為削弱權臣的實力，策劃「墮三都」，因此得罪號稱「三桓」的魯國卿大夫季孫氏、叔孫氏、孟孫氏。約略同時，齊國因懼孔子治魯成效出色將威脅齊國，贈魯君女樂文馬，設計使孔子與魯定公、季桓子等在道德政見上產生分歧，因而去魯適衛，開啟了輾轉於衞、曹、宋、鄭、陳、蔡、葉、楚等地，一共十四年周遊列國的旅程。（詳見孔子的足跡）

魯哀公十一年（西元前四八四年），季康子遣使以幣迎孔子歸魯，孔子為東南西北人的漂泊日子至此結束。但歸國後的孔子依舊未受魯君任用，轉將全副心神貫注於教學和整理古籍。翌年，獨子孔鯉先孔子而死，得年五十。魯哀公十四年（西元前四八一）西狩獲麟，一葉知秋的孔聖人以如此瑞應竟為亂世俗子所戮，哀嘆落淚，頹然停止編寫史書《春秋》。此年，孔子不唯痛失愛徒顏回，齊國陳恆弒君，孔子向魯君請求平亂遭拒，宰我因而與難。來年，忠耿勇武的子路慘死於一向混亂的衛國—接二連三的噩耗，使得周遊列國時即使畏於匡、被宋司馬桓魋伐樹追殺、過蒲歷險、厄於陳蔡，門外暴徒包圍，身後追兵將至，碗中絕糧多時，依舊充滿道德勇氣絃歌不絕的孔聖人相信，自己道窮，已失天眷，不再有機會一展抱負。

魯哀公十六年（西元前四七九年），孔子「夢坐奠於兩楹之間」，此為其祖殷人殯葬之禮，故告子貢曰己將死，之後寢病，七日而卒，終年七十三歲。葬於魯城北泗水岸邊，魯哀公尊之為「尼父」，眾多弟子以喪父禮守之。其中子貢廬墓六年，是他人之倍。據信，《論語》約略成於此時。2孔子的故所居堂，也被弟子保留為孔廟，保存其生前居所所用衣、冠、琴、車、書籍等供人瞻仰。3

雖然孔子在生時不受重用，無法一展理想抱負，但其謝世之後，卻倍極身後之榮。孔子故居成為門人習禮之所，歲時祭拜。漢高祖十二年（前一九五），漢高祖劉邦命大儒叔孫通據周禮制漢禮，平英布之亂返京，經由曲阜孔廟，以太牢祭孔。（見展件38《清沈振麟繪帝鑑圖說》）封孔子九代孫孔騰為「奉祀君」，專主孔子祀事；此舉不唯奠定後世天子以最高規格禮儀祭孔的典範，並且開例賜封孔氏嫡系長孫爵位俸祿，專司主祭之職。漢元帝元始元年（西元一年）追諡孔子為「褒成宣尼公」，孔子首度受封為公爵。漢明帝永平二年（五九），詔命祀先師孔子和先聖周公於太學及郡縣學，自此中央政府所在地，與各地方政府學校均舉辦祭孔儀式，祭孔成為全國性的重要活動。永平十五年（七二），漢明帝親自赴曲阜祭孔，且以七十二弟子從祀，愛屋及烏的擴增了祀奉對象。

此後，歷代追尊孔子的盛況，好比賽局加碼般更上層樓。唐玄宗開元二十七年（七三九）封孔子為「文宣王」，是孔子封王之始；且孔門重要弟子共有七十七人受贈公、侯、伯爵稱號。（見展件2－14《至聖先賢半身像冊》孔門諸弟子肖像）次年，詔春秋二仲丁日祭孔為大祀，舞用八佾舞，改公爵六佾舞，而成天子八佾之制。

到了宋代，追封孔子的競爭更趨白熱—北宋大中祥符元年

（一○○八）東封禮畢，宋真宗駕幸曲阜，在唐玄宗追諡孔子為「文

宣王」後，又為孔子加號「玄聖」，並「賜曲阜縣文宣王廟桓圭一，

從上公之制，冕九旒、服九章」；五年（一○一二）又因避聖祖趙玄

朗諱改為「至聖」文宣王，並且詔進封配享諸子；亦即一體同榮，所

有位列孔廟的門生都與老師同獲晉升封號的榮耀。神宗熙寧八年，右

正言常秩（一○一九－一○七七）建請孔子塑像用「天子之制十二旒

冕」，比真宗所封上公之制的九旒更進一等。

此後，大觀四年（一一一一），宋徽宗令「先聖廟用戟二十四，

文宣王執鎮圭，並如王者之制。」4 按唐開元以來禮制，一品官邸院

門前立戟數為十四，太廟、社、宮殿各施二十四戟。至此，孔廟立戟

之數已與皇帝宮殿等同。且以《周禮·春官》「王執鎮圭，公執桓圭」

的記載，徽宗賜孔子鎮圭，是符合其文宣「王」身分的持物，更勝真

宗所賜的桓圭為公爵之制。自此，孔子除了衣飾是比天子的十二章服

少了日、月、星辰三種的九章服以外，其他不只是稱號上封王，穿戴

與孔廟用度已經幾與皇帝等同。

雖然，孔子的漢族同族並沒有給孔子皇帝尊號，但西夏人慶三

年（同南宋紹興十六年，一一四六），倡議漢化文教的西夏仁宗頒

布詔令：「尊孔子為文宣帝，令州郡悉立廟祀，殿庭宏敞，並如帝

制。」5 孔子於是得到了道統上位極天下的皇帝稱號。金世宗大定年

間（一一六一－一一八九），亦將孔子的大成殿聖像穿戴定為等同皇

帝的「冠十二旒，服十二章」。明代，憲宗成化十三年（一四七七），

周洪謨請增孔廟禮樂，並定祭器籩豆數為十二，皆與天子制相等。6

清代，康熙二十三年（一六八四）聖祖親以三跪九叩的拜師大禮祭孔，

並創元首賜匾孔廟之例。7（見展件31清 聖祖 御筆書萬世師表）雍

正三年（一七二五），為避孔子諱，命天下丘姓子民改姓為「邱」，

並且世宗親自祭孔，也採跪姿獻帛進酒以示崇敬。8（詳見歷代封

祀孔子相關事蹟表）

綜觀前述各項，可以說在歷史上，孔子雖無皇帝之名，卻早已得

到了皇帝之實。並且，漢族以外的各民族統治者，往往在對孔子的崇

敬表現上更甚於漢族。先秦諸子百家之中，唯有老子因與大唐李氏同

姓，得到了玄元皇帝的封號。但孔姓子孫雖然無人在馬上得到天下，

歿世而名益顯的孔子卻在文治方面，超脫了改朝換代影響，得到了累

世天子的不斷追尊。

（二）繪畫中的孔子

根據孔子崇高地位所保留下來的相關記載，我們知道遠古時代，

中國即已有圖繪聖賢肖像的傳統。[9]但關於孔子的圖繪，卻不僅止於最基本的個人全身、半身肖像；而尚有各種經史故事性質的作品。此外，受到儒、釋、道三教融流的交互影響，孔子的生平事蹟，也被畫成了類似佛傳故事的《聖蹟圖》；以長卷、冊頁畫作，或是書籍中以版畫等形式流傳。[10]

存世孔子圖繪，以各種孔子個人肖像，與圖文對照的版畫聖蹟圖最多。並因孔門弟子眾多，書籍中多見孔子率領門生講學的插圖版畫；各地方志亦常有將孔子與重要弟子肖像畫在各處學校與廟堂之上，供學子觀看以生孺慕景仰的《禮殿圖》等記載。在選擇情節和取景方面，表現孔子好學不倦的問學態度，與誨人不厭講學行教身影的畫作，也都相當常見。由於本院藏品多單景式孔子像，本文重點，將聚焦於單景式展件介紹。

文獻記載的孔子特徵

文獻記載的孔子像極多，目前影響力最大，被歷代引用和模仿最多的孔子圖像，大概是現在曲阜孔府，據說出自唐代畫聖吳道子（約六八五－七五八）手筆的《先師孔子行教像》碑。（插圖一）然而，所有唐宋畫史著作，均無隻字記載吳道子曾作此像；並在線描與處理手法上，此畫線條也與記載中吳道子「蓴菜條」、「蘭葉描」、「吳帶當風」等風格頗有差距。[11]儘管疑點甚多，卻被中華民國孔孟協會與中華人民共和國孔子基金會所採信為吳生真蹟，而分別在一九八六年和二〇〇六年以此碑為藍本，繪制頒布所謂的「統一孔子像」和「孔子標準像」。這當然不是史上僅見的兩起意圖統一孔子像的事例─類似的事情也發生在明代。明太祖洪武年間（一三六八－一三九八），因認為某些孔子像無法確切展現孔子的偉大人格與神態，曾議令爾後新蓋孔廟，皆以牌位取代塑像，明世宗嘉靖年間（一五二二－一五六六），則更激烈的命令撤除全國孔子像，全以牌位祭祀，是為今日孔廟少見孔子塑像的原因。[12]

孔子長得甚麼樣？文獻對這方面的記載大致可以分為態度和樣貌兩類。一般認為《論語》是最親近孔子的弟子們所輯成，書中所

述應該最為可信。但如《論語·學而》，子貢描述「夫子溫良恭儉讓」，13以及《論語·述而》：「子溫而厲，威而不猛，恭而安。」14所提到的除了言談，都是孔子的表情、態度、舉止，而未言及五官相貌等特徵。

論孔子樣貌的，如荀況（約前三一三年－約前二三八年），在《荀子·非相》中提到：「仲尼長…仲尼之狀，面如蒙倛。」15說的是孔子身形偉岸，五官長相類似臘月趕鬼儀式中方相氏所用的面具。唐人楊倞注：「倛，方相也。其首蒙茸然，故曰蒙倛。」方相氏是周禮中的官職。掌蒙熊皮、黃金四目、玄衣朱裳、執戈揚盾為國家驅疫，此一方相氏驅疫的儀式叫大儺，唐朝成為為軍禮之一，每年有三次，分別於季春、仲秋、季冬。除夕夜逐疫是最隆重的一次。日本奈良時代（七一〇－七九四）以前，儺從中國傳入日本，叫做追儺式，很多神道教神社每年除夕和立春均會舉辦。本院所藏傳《宋蘇漢臣畫五瑞圖》中，（插圖二）聚戲庭中的五位童子，即是戴著假面或塗臉化妝，在進行以大儺舞為主題的遊戲。大儺原為古代驅邪習俗，後演變為民間娛樂活動。推測此圖右下角手執笏版者，所戴面具即為蒙倛。楊倞對荀子「面如蒙倛」的解釋「其首蒙茸然」，或許即為後世孔子像皆鬚髯豐茂，闊面濃眉的特徵所據。

莊周（約前三六九－約前二八六），《莊子·外物》的相關記載有：「老萊子之弟子出薪，遇仲尼，反以告，曰：『有人於彼，修上而趨下，末僂而後耳，視若營四海，不知其誰氏之子。』老萊子曰：『是丘也。召而來。』」16提到孔子的上下身比例、略為駝背的姿勢、有點後貼或後反的耳朵，和如若經營四海的眼神。西漢司馬遷，《史記·孔子世家》對孔子樣貌的形容為：「生而首上圩頂，故因名曰丘云……孔子長九尺六寸，人皆謂之『長人』而異之……孔子適鄭，

與弟子相失，孔子獨立郭東門。鄭人或謂子貢曰：『東門有人，其顙
似堯，其項類皋陶，其肩類子產，然自要以下不及禹三寸……』」[17]
記錄了孔子的具體身高，與鄭人對子貢形容孔子的言論。另託名秦漢
之際孔子九世孫孔鮒（約活動於西元前三世紀）所撰的《孔叢子》，
記載孔子適周訪樂，音樂家萇弘（？—前四九二年）對他的形容是：
「吾觀孔仲尼有聖人之表，河目而隆顙……修肱而龜背，長九尺有六
寸……」[18]除了身高外，還類比形容了孔子眼睛、額頭、手臂、背型。

唐代司馬貞（約六七九—約七三三）《史記索隱》記，西漢景
帝（西元前一五一—前一四一在位）時，蜀郡太守文翁曾圖孔子及
弟子七十二人[19]。然此記載已是唐代二手資料，或未可信。目前已
知最早為孔子畫像的文獻記載，是《三國志·倉慈傳》記東漢桓帝
時（一四七—一六七）在老子廟壁上畫《孔子像》[20]，以及《後漢
書·蔡邕傳》，靈帝光和元年（一七八），「置鴻都門學，畫孔子及
七十二弟子像」[21]，以上圖繪記載，都已經是孔子謝世之後六百多年
的事情。

考古出土的孔子形象

考古資料顯示，「孔子見老子」是東漢時期畫像石最常出現的
題材之一，其中最為著名的，是建於東漢桓帝建和元年（一四七），
山東嘉祥武氏祠中出土的〈孔子見老子〉畫像石（插圖三）；時間約
在東漢桓帝、靈帝時期（一四七—一八八），內蒙古和林格爾漢墓的
〈孔子見老子〉壁畫（插圖四）；以及時代落在西漢晚期至東漢早期
（約西元一世紀）山東東平漢墓壁畫（插圖五）。另外，二〇一一—
二〇一五年發掘江西南昌海昏侯劉賀（西元前九二—前五九年）墓葬
所出土，上具孔子生平介紹文字的屏風狀孔子圖像穿衣鏡，則可將繪
製孔子像的時間更向前提早到西漢時代。

如今可見漢代畫像石與壁畫中的孔子形象，大多強調其人身形高
大，動作謙遜的特徵，即《荀子》、《史記》等記載的「仲尼長」、
「孔子長九尺六寸」的外表身高，以及《論語》「溫良恭儉讓」、「溫
而厲，威而不猛，恭而安」等內在精神氣質，其後所見的孔子像基本
皆繼承了以上兩大原則。

本次選展畫作

根據文獻記載，晉王廙（二七六—三三二）、戴逵（約三三一—
三九六）、顧愷之（約三四五—四〇六）、宗炳（三七五—四四
三），南朝梁張僧繇（約活動於西元五至六世紀）、陸探微（？—約
四八五）、劉瑱（約四六〇—五〇一）、梁元帝蕭繹（五〇八—
五五五）和唐代周昉（約活動於八—九世紀）、閻立本（？—

插圖三、山東嘉祥武梁祠〈孔子見老子〉畫像石　取自秦明，《蓬萊宿約：故宮藏黃易漢魏碑刻特集》頁一五二。

插圖四、內蒙古和林格爾漢墓〈孔子見老子〉壁畫　取自內蒙古自治區博物館文物工作隊《和林格爾漢墓壁畫》頁一三八。

六七三）、王維（七○一－七六一）、董源（約活動於十世紀）、梁楷（約活動於十三世紀）等著名畫家都曾以孔子像為題材進行創作，可惜至今皆未有可信實物留存。22

雖然如此，參照諸多現存文物，仍可發現歷代所接受認可的孔子像，均具有類似的特徵，畫面中的孔子往往是一鬚髯豐茂，神態恭謙，身著布袍，腰配長劍，年約六七十歲的暮年老者。全身立像者，如本展所選《聖君賢臣全身像冊》（展件18）孔子，以水墨畫，線條勻稱，流暢細勁，衣褶以墨暈染，意甚高古。圖中孔子長眉垂鬚，端正站立，姿態略躬，似以示敬，神色安詳，以表好禮。全身坐像如傳〈宋高宗書孝經馬和之繪圖 冊 開宗明義章〉（展件15）與〈明文徵明楷書孝經仇英畫〉（展件16），畫孔子端坐樹下，為曾子講述孝經。二畫中的孔子皆左手撫膝，舉右手欲言，只是前者孔子雙頰瘦削，額頭、眼角與鼻翼多畫皺紋，面色略微黝黑，顯出老態；後者則豐頰廣頤，面貌光潤，容色白皙，看起來較為年輕而有精神。另一系列的孔子全身坐像則手有持物，如《聖賢像贊》與《聖廟祀典圖攷》書中的孔子坐像版畫（展件20、19），均繪濃眉豐髯的孔子，冠服端整，持笏正坐。此見《禮記·玉藻》：「笏，天子以球玉，諸侯以象，大夫以魚須文竹，士竹，本，象可也……凡有指畫於君前，用笏；造受命於君前，則書於笏。笏，畢用也，因飾焉。」依古禮制，諸侯士大夫須持笏見天子，在天子面前若需指畫，則以笏為之。此二孔子持笏坐像所繪，則應為孔子在廟堂之上為天子陳述政事的情形，推測是後世為彰顯孔子身為王者之師與天子之師所做的構圖安排。

　另有《至聖先賢半身像冊》的孔子（展件1），以重彩設色畫由頭頂至胸的孔子特寫肖像。此冊原藏於清宮安奉歷代帝后賢臣圖像的「南薰殿」，按照題籤封號，可知繪製時間在元文宗至順元年（一三三〇）追封孔子各大弟子公爵之位以後。此圖孔子已經加入膚黑與七露的神性化特徵。膚黑疑為北宋真宗一度為孔子所加「玄聖」封號所造成的影響。23活動於兩宋之交的孔子四十六世孫孔傳（約活動於十一至十二世紀），所撰《東家雜記・孔子追封諡號》，記述「玄聖文宣王」封號，是因為漢代充滿神話迷信色彩的緯書《春秋孔演圖》曰『孔子母感黑帝而生』……故有是號。」推測宋真宗以孔子是屬於黑帝的殷商王室後裔，故加孔子以具有黑色意涵的「玄聖」封號。而崇尚聖人受到天命感生，故而反映在外貌異表的思想，可能在某種程度上影響了畫家對孔子形貌的理解，故而在孔子膚色方面，做出了偏黑的神話性處理。24七露則見宋代相書《太清神鑑》：「眼睛露，黑白分明不為露；鼻露竅，山根正不為露；口露齒，唇不褰不為露；耳反輪，貼肉生不為露」。25所謂七露，是指眼、耳、鼻、口四官七竅，讓人一望可見的部分較多。相書所謂的露而不為露，因為敗中有救，是吉人貴相的要素。此冊孔子眼睛瞳仁部分重複點睛，與傳說中帝舜重瞳的特徵相符，構思所據，推測是收入西漢文帝景帝（西元前

一七九－前一四一年）時人韓嬰所著《韓詩外傳》卷九，春秋時期著名的相士姑布子卿告訴子貢孔子「得舜之目」的記載。26

　目前所見孔子像，除問學、恭立、端坐、講示以外，其餘常見者尚有以鼓琴為主題者。孔子受樂、眾人皆知。他曾訪樂萇弘、學琴師襄，27在齊聞韶，三月不知肉味；與人歌而善，必使反之，而後和之。即使遭厄於陳蔡之間，絕糧七日，弟子餒病，孔子依舊絃歌不輟。《宋人畫歷代琴式圖　冊》以水墨畫歷代帝王與古聖賢琴式，每幅上方並錄相關故實一則，共三十一幅，琴式命名的方式，反映了古人對聖賢、帝王和文人的推崇。本次選展〈孔子之制〉，畫孔子端坐於瀑崖樹下，膝上橫琴，兩手撫弦。雙目右視，似正注意著彈撥琴弦的右手。古琴亦稱七弦琴，孔子時代即已盛行，是中國最古老的樂器之一。琴體腰與頸部方折凹入，通體線條流暢的仲尼琴式，是唐宋以來最常見的古琴種類，至今依舊是最為流行的古琴款式。其餘，線描版畫中的孔子圖像，也有展現孔子為求甚解，不思躁進，非常認真的捲起袖子低頭彈琴，極為投入而賣力的表現。（見展件21《清聖廟祀典圖攷　學琴師襄〉）

　孔子雖然故去已有兩千餘年，而其精神思想卻百代不朽。關於孔子形貌最初的記載，僅只是身高過人，卻因為後世對他的景仰，為孔子的樣貌加入了不少神話傳奇性質的異表元素。到了孔子第五十一代孫，金元時期人孔元措（一一八二－約一二五二）所著《孔氏祖庭廣

記》，對於「先聖小像」的描述已經非常接近於佛陀三十二相、八十種好。28歷代畫作對於孔子形貌的構思處理，多半繪其濃眉多髯；對於動作的選取安排，則一定意圖表現孔子的好學多禮與端謹謙恭。現存的孔子肖像，所畫絕大部分都是中老年時期的孔子，即便後人考據，孔子學琴師襄是三十歲左右，現存畫作中的孔子也都是鬚長掩頸，看起來老成持重的壯年人。或許可說這些孔子像雖然未必真的能夠詳實肖似孔子的面容，但所呈現的卻是歷代人民心目中對孔子樣貌的認同與想像。

（三）與孔子相關的書法作品

儒家教育要求的君子六藝是「禮、樂、射、御、書、數」，中國的書法原本就是一門極具文人情態的藝術。對於歷代文人來說，孔子是思想上的一代宗師，兼具文人身分的書法家述及孔子師弟及儒家思想的作品在所多見，其中名品如唐代歐陽詢（五五七－六四一）的〈卜商帖〉（插圖六）及〈仲尼夢奠帖〉（插圖七）均屬其類。對歷代政權來說，孔子強調的仁義忠孝思想則是穩定社會的力量。尊孔修廟是值得刻石記功的大事，碑文的撰文者和書寫者經常都是一時之選不說，對自己書法有自信的帝王還會親筆御書碑區頒賜孔廟。（展件31）除此以外，孔氏家學淵源，加以帝王尊孔崇聖特意拔擢，也使得孔姓子孫的行狀墓誌頗有可觀。與孔子相關的書法名作，大致可以分為以下數類：與孔子相關者、與孔廟相關者、與太學相關者，以下將分別概述。（詳院藏孔子相關書法）

託名孔子的書作

現存曾被歸為孔子名下的書法，有現在河南比干廟的〈魯司寇孔丘延陵帖〉（插圖八），與收入《淳化閣法帖》、《宋拓大觀帖》、《明拓寶賢堂集古法帖冊》、《清乾隆御製重刻淳化閣帖等》的〈魯司寇孔丘延陵帖〉（插圖九）。然〈殷比干墓〉為隸書，絕非孔子時文字，而應為漢代之人所書。29另外，雖然自唐代以來，世傳〈魯司寇孔丘延陵帖〉為孔子替史稱「延陵季子」的吳國賢人季札（約活動於西元前六世紀）墓碑書篆之作，然宋歐陽修（一〇〇七－一〇七二）以孔子「歷聘諸侯，南不逾楚」，未曾到過吳國，亦不可能替季子書碑；並且此書原石字大徑尺，「非簡牘所容」；元代盛熙明（約活動於十四世紀），《法書考》也記錄，此作篆法中夾有漢代方篆筆法，亦疑此為漢代以前之人託名題墓。30

孔廟漢隸名品與〈孔氏子孫碑刻〉

雖然，今世孔子手蹟已然不存，但世間確實存在著大量與孔子有

156

關的書法名作。並且數量之龐大，位置之集中，可以說是古今中外所少見。

因崇聖之故一直未遭劫火的曲阜孔廟，與保有唐代長安國子監石經的西安，有著中國最有名的兩大碑林，在此二處保存下來眾多自漢以來的碑刻名品，碑文內容主旨集中在修建孔廟、崇儒興學、刻經搨碑、獎尚文治，以及歷代帝王與地方官員士紳等，對孔子及其弟子的祭祀與追諡等。

插圖八、河南衛縣比干廟刻石　取自河南新鄉比干廟旅遊網頁

其中最為著稱者，當以漢碑名品，被稱為「孔廟三碑」的〈乙瑛碑〉、〈禮器碑〉與〈史晨碑〉為首（展件24、25、26）。按刻碑年代先後，碑文端謹肅穆，被清人推為漢隸典型的東漢永興元年（一五三）立〈乙瑛碑〉，記魯前相乙瑛等奏聞，孔子十九世孫孔麟，請依漢代祠廟定制，設立百石卒史，負責孔廟禮器、春秋祭典各項禮儀，後訪得賢者孔龢擔任始末。被譽為東漢碑刻書法經典，碑文運筆變化多端，神采超然的永壽二年（一五六）〈禮器碑〉，

記魯相韓敕修整孔廟、置辦禮器和吏民共同捐資立石頌德事。另筆法溫和蘊藉，氣勢沉古遒厚，分別刻於東漢靈帝建寧二年（一六九）與建寧元年（一六八）的前後〈史晨碑〉，則記魯相史晨到官時拜祭孔子並上書奏請每年春秋兩季行祭孔之禮。清人王澍（一六六八－一七三九）在《虛舟題跋》中，對此三碑的評價與臨學次第提出：「史晨嚴謹，始立根基；乙瑛雄古，繼究其大；禮器變化，終盡其變。」以上三碑現均在曲阜，皆為東漢孔廟草創階段的重要碑刻，同時也因為是漢隸學習範本，對於後世書學影響極其深長。

除了對於書學的影響以外，以上三碑其實也提供了許多早期的孔廟祭孔相關資訊。例如〈乙瑛碑〉提及「出王家錢給犬酒」、「河南尹給牛羊豕雞□□各一。大司農給米」，等祭品出處。〈禮器碑〉述及孔子母族顏氏，與妻族「并官氏」，目前常見孔子妻「亓官氏」，但宋代《通志》與明以前姓氏考證類書則均為「并官氏」，或許其中在明代以後有誤傳情況待考。〈史晨碑〉後碑所述之「河東大守孔彪元上」，即顏書所祖東漢建寧四年（一七一）立，筆畫精勁，結構謹嚴，向列漢隸名品之一的〈孔彪碑〉碑主；亦是東漢桓帝延禧七年（一六四）所立，以流麗華美書法知名的〈孔宙碑〉碑主孔融（一五三－二〇八）父孔宙之弟，均為孔子第十九代聖裔。清乾隆五十八年（一七九三）發現於孔子墓圍牆外的永壽元年（一五五）〈孔君墓碣〉，也可由官職得知此為孔子十九世孫孔少垂墓碣，此

作隸法亦淳厚蒼勁，可供取法。

漢代朝廷對於「世以家學相承，自為師友」的孔氏一門極為優禮，其族貴盛顯赫，為官樹政，常見立碑流芳事例。孔宙共有七子，除孔融以外，《孔謙碣》碑主孔謙，字德讓，其碑立於東漢永興二年（一五四），隸書字體雍容莊重，波磔較長。七兄弟中還有孔褒（？－一六九，一作孔曜，字文禮）之碑，書體嚴整，書風蒼厚。雍正三年（一七二五）鄉民犁田時出土，隨即移入曲阜孔廟。以上孔氏子孫的紀念刻石，在後世都成為了金石考證與書法家的參考依據。

孔廟的刻石銘記

自從漢高祖劉邦太牢祭孔，成為後世帝王典範之後，歷代意圖標榜自身賢明的帝王無不以具體的追封孔子和修建孔廟來表彰對道統的崇敬。例如書法史上赫赫有名之作，唐貞觀七年（六三三）所立的《虞世南夫子廟堂碑》，即是記載唐高祖封孔子二十三世後裔孔德倫為褒聖侯，並修孔廟之事。此碑碑文為歷代公認的初唐碑刻傑作，也為著名書法家虞世南（五五八－六三八）保留了一件，用筆淳熟含蓄，氣象雅潤平和的書法妙品。

曲阜地近歷代封禪祭拜天地所在的泰山，或許由於東周稷下學宮彼此影響的原故，齊魯儒士認為泰山是天下最高的山，受命於天的人間帝王應到此山祭神。後來在齊、魯祭祀泰山的儀式，擴大為統一帝國「封禪」儀式。而歷代統治者為了表達對孔子的尊崇，

插圖九、傳春秋仲尼延陵帖 《宋搨大觀帖》 國立故宮博物院藏

行程安排上往往在封禪泰山之後，幸駕曲阜。孔廟在帝王不時親臨的情況之下，屢屢奉旨修繕，並且刻石立碑。如北宋大中祥符五年（一○一二）《真宗御製玄聖文宣王贊碑》，所記即為大中祥符年間宋真宗趙恆（九六八－一○二二）駕幸曲阜，封孔子為玄聖文宣王，並且詔進封配享諸子之事。

除了皇帝降旨以外，一般官員仕紳也常因為崇尚文教，以集資或捐獻的方式籌款修建孔廟。例如東魏孝靜帝興和三年（五四一），兗州刺史李珽塑孔子及十弟子像，立了《魏李仲璇修孔子廟碑》，這是目前已知最早為孔子和孔門十哲塑像的記載，也反映了當時個體間雜並且大量使用異體字的書藝風尚。（展件28）

其他較為著名者，還有隋大業七年（六一一）《陳叔毅修孔子廟碑》，是記陳宣帝之子陳叔毅擔任曲阜縣令時，重修曲阜孔廟的始末碑刻；唐大曆八年（七七三）《裴孝智撰文宣王廟門記》敘述大曆八年（七七三）兗州刺史孟休鑒、曲阜縣令裴有象新建曲阜孔廟廟門事蹟。碑文展現了中唐楷法入隸的書風；以及筆畫瘦勁，具柳公權書法清朗風貌，可窺晚唐楷書趨向的《曲阜文宣王廟記》，碑記唐咸通十一年（八七○）孔子第三十九世孫孔溫裕奏准出個人薪資修繕孔廟，獲得朝廷嘉獎始末。以上三碑原石現皆存於山東曲阜孔廟，都是書法史上相當重要的刻石。

另在至今少見的西漢隸書當中，最為有名的五鳳二年（西元前五六）「漢魯孝王刻石」，也是金章宗明昌二年（一一九一）重修曲阜孔廟時，自魯靈光殿址西南釣魚池石塊中發現的。作為文人聖殿的孔廟，也有書家起題字雅興而揮毫，如原位於孔子手植檜側的北宋崇寧二年（一一○三）《米芾孔子手植檜贊》等，曲阜孔廟似乎因其特殊情況，聚集並且發現了不少歷代石碑。

廟學合一與太學石經

孔子畢生致力於教育，在其身後，子孫即宅為廟，藏本服禮器，世以家學相承，自為師友，而魯之諸生，亦時習禮其家。此舉奠定了中國教育史上「即廟設學」的特色，如今所見民國以前縣級以上的孔廟，多屬當時學校的一部分。五經既為孔子所述，學校師生皆可謂是孔子的再傳弟子，這種「廟學合一」的情況，也促成了「學祭合一」，使學校主辦，令學子們參與春秋兩季釋奠祭儀。

在朝廷支持，寓政於教的背景下，刻定石經，以正傳抄之謬是相當重要的文教大事，此事始自東漢靈帝熹平四年（一七五）至光和六年（一八三），學界領袖及書法家蔡邕親自書丹於碑，使工鑴刻《魯詩》、《周易》、《尚書》、《儀禮》、《春秋》、《公羊傳》及《論語》七經，共四十六石立於太學門外。此後亦有三國魏正始二年（二四一）

以古文、小篆與隸書三體刻《正始石經》；唐代天寶四年（七四五），玄宗曾御筆書寫《石臺孝經》。唐文宗時又以標準唐楷刻《周易》、《尚書》、《毛詩》、三禮、春秋三傳、《孝經》、《論語》、《爾雅》等儒家經書十二種，共一百一十四石，立於長安國子監，因完工於開成二年（八三七），史稱《開成石經》。此經在北宋時曾因數次遷徙以避戰禍，形成了後來的西安碑林。其後刻立石經的事例，尚有五代十國後蜀廣政年間（九五一~九五八）所刻《廣政石經》、北宋仁宗嘉祐元年（一〇五六）至六年（一〇六一）以楷書與小篆二體刻的《汴學石經》、南宋紹興十三年（一一四三）高宗趙構御筆親書，立於太學的《紹興石經》，以及清代乾隆五十九年（一七九四）刻江蘇金壇蔣衡（一六七二~一七四三）費時十二年所抄十三經以成六十多萬字的《乾隆石經》。

孔子看似與書法無關，但傳統文化上的文字與典故中，孔子所造成的影響處處可見。不只是原本傳承四書五經長安國子學的西安碑林，和曲阜的孔廟碑林，保存了諸多漢唐時代的早期名作；而孔子的子孫、孔廟修繕與祭儀、孔門弟子，如第一高足顏回的《兗公頌碑》和北京故宮所藏的《唐歐陽詢卜商帖》等，都可說是孔子師生與孔子世系間接影響，無心插柳所留下的書法藝術。

《孔子世家》最末寫道：「天下君王至於賢人眾矣，當時則榮，沒則已焉。孔子布衣，傳十餘世，學者宗之。自天子王侯，中國言六藝者折中於夫子，可謂至聖矣。」早在唐玄宗封孔子為王之前八百多年，太史公司馬遷即已將布衣平民的孔子列入諸侯王者等級的「世家」當中。

孔子歿世而名稱，在中國歷史上，沒有任何一個帝王將相或風雲人物能達到他的影響力。代代圖其形貌者不絕於朝野，其言其事更因鑴鏤金石而得以長存，即使不斷地以誇示性手法添加諸多不同於常人的神話異表，也依舊不減他「聖之時者」歷久不衰的學思理想。

康熙二十三年（一六八四），清聖祖南巡，親至曲阜孔子故居，賜御筆「萬世師表」榜書，懸於大成殿中。翌年，下詔頒發此蹟摹本發送天下文廟。如今，在全臺首學臺南孔廟，依舊高懸著這麼一幅藍底金字，沉厚蒼勁的「萬世師表」。昂藏於清代與民國歷任元首的贈匾之間，它仍是臺南孔廟時代最早、面積最大的一塊匾額；而「萬世師表」四字也早已成為孔子的最佳代稱。至於原本康熙御筆的下落，多年以來無人知曉。此匾的墨書原蹟，一度被以為已經燒毀在文化大革命的烈火當中；實則被孔子的第七十七代嫡長孫孔德成（一九二〇~二〇〇八）先生低調的護送來台，獻藏國立故宮博物院。

本次展覽，最初肇因於筆者偶然發現院藏墨拓碑刻中與孔子、孔廟相關者極多，加以清宮舊藏南薰殿圖像亦有孔子全身及半身肖像，故開始策劃此展。籌辦期間，幸蒙書畫處劉處長芳如告知康熙御筆「萬世師表」墨蹟現藏本院，因而以此亮點作為展名。至於孔府護寶無私的精神，筆者不勝感動敬佩之心，謹於此處誠摯申謝。

註釋：

1 羊春秋，《本姓解第九十三》，《新譯孔子家語》，臺北：三民書局，一九九六。

2 （漢）班固，《漢書·藝文志》：「論語者，孔子應答弟子、時人，及弟子相與言而接聞於夫子之語也。當時弟子各有所記，夫子既卒，門人相與輯而論撰，故謂之論語。」

3 （漢）司馬遷，《史記》（景印文淵閣四庫全書，二四四冊，二三三一~二五二頁），卷四十七，〈孔子世家〉，頁三五。

4 （宋），馬端臨，《文獻通考》，《學校考五·祠祭褒贈先聖先師》（景印文淵閣四庫全書，六一一冊，五六~七六頁），

5 （元），脫脫，《宋史》（景印文淵閣四庫全書，二八八冊，七六七~七八一頁），卷四百八十六，〈列傳第二百四十五·外國二·夏國下〉，頁二四。

6 （清）谷應泰，《明史紀事本末》（景印文淵閣四庫全書，三六四

7 陳芳妹，〈臺南孔廟「萬世師表」御匾—兼論康熙與清初孔廟御匾制度的形成及傳播〉，《故宮學術季刊》，三一卷一期（二〇一三），頁一九九~二三〇。

8 （清），《世宗憲皇帝聖訓》（景印文淵閣四庫全書，四一二冊，一一頁），卷一，〈聖德一〉，頁一二。

9 見《孔子家語·觀周第十一》：「孔子觀乎明堂，觀四門墉有堯舜與桀紂之象，而各有善惡之狀、興廢之誡焉；；又有周公相成王，抱之負斧扆南面以朝諸侯之圖焉。」且後註十五中，鄭人對子貢形容孔子樣貌時，非常具體的與堯、皋陶、子產、禹等人的特徵相提並論，可見當時必有圖繪古代聖賢肖像的處所。

10 許瑜翎，《明代孔子「聖蹟圖」研究—以傳世正統九年本《聖蹟圖》為中心》（台北：國立台灣師範大學碩士論文，二〇一〇）。

11 （宋）郭若虛，《圖畫見聞誌》（景印文淵閣四庫全書，八一二冊，五一五頁），卷一，〈論曹吳體法〉，頁一三三。

12 吳靜芳，〈明嘉靖孔廟祀典改制考析〉，《成大歷史學報》，第三十一號（二〇〇六），頁一二三~一五二。

13 （魏）何晏，《論語集解義疏》（景印文淵閣四庫全書，一九五冊，三四五頁），卷一，〈學而第一〉，頁一二。

14 同上註，卷四，〈述而第七〉，頁二三三。

15 （周）荀況，《荀子》（景印文淵閣四庫全書，六九五冊，一三九~一四〇頁），卷三，〈非相〉，頁一一二。

冊，六三四頁），卷五十一，〈更定祀典上〉，頁九。

16（晉）郭象，《莊子注》（景印文淵閣四庫全書，一○五六冊，一三七―一三八頁），卷九，〈外物〉，頁三―四。

17 同註三，頁二―一六。

18（漢）孔鮒，《孔叢子》（景印文淵閣四庫全書，六九五冊，三一○頁），卷上，〈嘉言第一〉，頁一。

19（唐）司馬貞，《史記索隱》（景印文淵閣四庫全書，二四六冊，五六五頁），卷十八，〈仲尼弟子列傳第十七〉，頁一。

20（魏）陳壽，《三國志》（景印文淵閣四庫全書，二五四冊，三三四頁），卷一六，〈倉慈傳〉，頁三○。

21（唐）張彥遠，《歷代名畫記》（景印文淵閣四庫全書，八一二冊，三一五頁），卷四，〈外物〉，頁三：「劉旦、楊魯、並光和中畫手，待詔尚方，畫於洪都學。」

22 孔德平，〈歷代孔子造像述略〉，《中華文化畫報》，二○○七年第八期。

23 詳見徐興無，〈作為匹夫的玄聖素王―讖緯文獻中的孔子形象與思想〉，收在黃俊傑編，《東亞論語學：中國篇》（臺北，臺灣大學出版中心，二○○九），頁一三九―一六八。高明一，〈至聖文宣王：孔子在北宋的尊崇與形象〉，《故宮文物月刊》四二二期（二○一七‧○七）待刊稿。

24 詳細的分析，見徐興無，〈作為匹夫的玄聖素王―讖緯文獻中的孔子形象與思想〉，收在黃俊傑編，《東亞論語學：中國篇》（臺北，臺灣大學出版中心，二○○九），頁一三九―一六八。

25（宋），不詳作者，《太清神鑑》，（景印文淵閣四庫全書，

26（漢）韓嬰，《韓詩外傳》（景印文淵閣四庫全書八九冊，八五○頁），卷九，〈嘉言第一〉，頁八―九：「子貢曰：『賜之師何如？』姑布子卿曰：『得堯之顙，舜之目，禹之頸，皋陶之喙。從前視之，盎盎乎似有王者；從後視之，高肩弱脊，此惟不及四聖者也。』子貢吁然。姑布子卿曰：『何患焉。汙面而不惡，葭喙而不藉，遠而望之，羸乎若喪家之狗，子何患焉！子何患焉！』

27（魏）王肅，《孔子家語》（景印文淵閣四庫全書，六九五冊，七八頁），卷八，〈辨樂解第三十五〉，頁五：「孔子學琴於師襄子。襄子曰：『吾雖以擊磬為官，然能於琴，今子於琴已習，可以益矣。』孔子曰：『丘未得其數也。』有間，曰：『已習其數，可以益矣。』孔子曰：『丘未得其志也。』有間，曰：『已習其志，可以益矣。』孔子曰：『丘未得其為人也。』有間，孔子有所繆然思焉，有所睪然高望而遠眺，曰：『丘迨得其為人矣。近黮而黑，頎然長，曠如望羊，奄有四方，非文王其孰能為此？』師襄子避席葉拱而對曰：『君子聖人也！其傳曰：《文王操》。』」

28（金）孔元措，《孔氏祖庭廣記》，卷八，〈先聖小像〉：「《家譜云，先聖長九尺六寸，腰大十圍，凡四十九表：反首洼面，月角日準，手握天文，足履度字，或作王字。坐如龍蹲，立如鳳峙，望之如仆，就之如升，耳垂殊庭，龜脊龍形，參膺河目，海口山臍，林背翼臂，斗唇注頭，隆鼻阜脥，堤眉地足，谷竅雷聲，澤腹昌顏，均頤輔喉，駢齒眉有一十二采，目有六十四理，其頭似陶唐，其顙似虞舜，其項類皋陶，其肩類子產，自腰以下不及禹三寸…」

29（清）顧藹吉，《隸辨》，（景印文淵閣四庫全書，二三五冊，八○○頁），卷八，〈碑攷下〉，頁三二一―三二三。

30（元）盛熙明，《法書考》，（景印文淵閣四庫全書，八一四，四九八頁），卷一，〈延陵君子碑〉，頁三七－三八。

31（清）王澍，《竹雲題跋》，（景印文淵閣四庫全書，六八四冊，六四五頁），卷一，〈延陵季子墓題字〉，頁一－三。

參考書目：

一、古籍文獻

（周）荀況，《荀子》，收入《文淵閣四庫全書》，第六九五冊，臺北：台灣商務印書館，一九八三。

（漢）孔鮒，《孔叢子》，收入《文淵閣四庫全書》，第六九五冊，臺北：台灣商務印書館，一九八三。

（漢）司馬遷，《史記》，收入《文淵閣四庫全書》，第二四四冊，臺北：台灣商務印書館，一九八三。

（漢）班固，《漢書·藝文志》，臺北：新文豐，一九八五。

（漢）韓嬰，《韓詩外傳》，收入《文淵閣四庫全書》，第八九冊，臺北：台灣商務印書館，一九八三。

（唐）司馬貞，《史記索隱》，收入《文淵閣四庫全書》，第五六五冊，臺北：台灣商務印書館，一九八三。

（魏）何晏，《論語集解義疏》，收入《文淵閣四庫全書》，第一九五冊，臺北：台灣商務印書館，一九八三。

（魏）陳壽，《三國志》，收入《文淵閣四庫全書》，第二五四冊，臺北：台灣商務印書館，一九八三。

（魏）王肅，《孔子家語》，收入《文淵閣四庫全書》，第六九五冊，臺北：台灣商務印書館，一九八三。

（晉）郭象，《莊子注》，收入《文淵閣四庫全書》，第一〇五六冊，臺北：台灣商務印書館，一九八五。

（唐）張彥遠，《歷代名畫記》，收入《文淵閣四庫全書》，第八一二冊，臺北：台灣商務印書館，一九八三。

（宋）不詳作者，《太清神鑑》，收入《文淵閣四庫全書》，第八一〇冊，臺北：台灣商務印書館，一九八三。

（宋）胡仔，《孔子編年》，北京：北京圖書館出版社，一九九九。

（宋）馬端臨，《文獻通考》，〈學校考五·祠祭褒贈先聖先師〉，收入《文淵閣四庫全書》，第六一一冊，臺北：台灣商務印書館，一九八三。

（宋）郭若虛，《圖畫見聞誌》，收入《文淵閣四庫全書》，第八一二冊，臺北：台灣商務印書館，一九八三。

（元）脫脫，《宋史》，收入《文淵閣四庫全書》，第二八八冊，臺北：台灣商務印書館，一九八三。

（元）盛熙明，《法書考》，收入《文淵閣四庫全書》，第八一四冊，臺北：台灣商務印書館，一九八三。

（金）孔元措，《孔氏祖庭廣記》，臺北：藝文出版社，一九六七。

（明）張居正、呂調陽，《帝鑑圖說》，哈爾濱：哈爾濱出版社，二〇〇九。

（明）沈繼震，《孔子年譜》，北京：北京圖書館出版社，一九九九。

（清）杜詔，《孔子年譜》，北京：北京圖書館出版社，一九九九。

（清）《滿漢繙譯四書》，臺北市：中國邊疆歷史語文學會，一九六八。

（清）蔣元樞纂輯，《重修臺郡各建築圖說》，臺北：國立故宮博物院，二〇〇七。

（清）張照、梁詩正等奉敕撰，《石渠寶笈》，收入《文淵閣四庫全書》，第八二四冊，臺北：台灣商務印書館，一九八三。

（清）清聖祖御製，《聖祖仁皇帝庭訓格言》，收入《文淵閣四庫全書》，第七一七冊，臺北：台灣商務印書館，一九八三。

（清）清聖祖御製，《聖祖仁皇帝御製文集》，收入《文淵閣四庫全書》，第一二九九冊，臺北：台灣商務印書館，一九八三。

（清）《世宗憲皇帝聖訓》，收入《文淵閣四庫全書》，第四一二冊，臺北：台灣商務印書館，一九八三。

（清）孔繼汾《闕里文獻考》，臺北：維新書局，一九六八。

（清）谷應泰，《明史紀事本末》，收入《文淵閣四庫全書》，第三六四冊，臺北：台灣商務印書館，一九八三。

（清）顧藹吉，《隸辨》，收入《文淵閣四庫全書》，第二三五冊，臺北：台灣商務印書館，一九八三。

（清）王澍，《竹雲題跋》，收入《文淵閣四庫全書》，第六八四冊，臺北：台灣商務印書館，一九八三。

二、近代論著

瀧川龜太郎，《史記會注考證》，臺北：中新書局，一九七七。

羽田亨，《滿和辭典》，臺北：學海出版社，二〇一一。

安雙成主編，《滿漢大辭典》，朝陽：遼寧民族出版社，一九九三。

陳舜臣、近藤喬一、町田三郎，《山東省文物「孔子の原鄉四千年展」》，東京：讀賣新聞，一九九二。

莊吉發，《龍章鳳藻鐵畫銀鈎一清聖祖論書法》，《故宮文物月刊》，一九九二年六月，一一一期，頁一一二-一二七。

陳捷先，《清聖祖與書法》，《故宮學術季刊》，卷一七（期一，一九九九年秋季），頁一-一八。

楊丹霞，《試論清康熙帝書法的淵源、分期與影響》，《故宮博物院院刊》，二〇〇八年第五期，頁八九-一〇四。

何炎泉，《萬幾餘暇怡情翰墨—從三件院藏品看清聖祖書法及其書學》，《故宮文物月刊》，二〇一一年十一月，三四四期，頁四〇-四九。

許文美、劉芳如，《明四大家特展—仇英》，臺北：國立故宮博物院，二〇一四。

許仁圖、愛新覺羅·毓鋆，《子曰論語》，臺北：河洛圖書出版社，二〇一一。

黃俊傑編，《東亞視域中孔子的形象與思想》，臺北：臺大出版中心，二○一五。

閻韜，《孔子與儒家》，臺北：臺灣商務印書館，二○○三。

白川靜，《孔子》，臺北：聯經，二○一六。

陳芳妹，《青銅器與宋代文化史》，臺北：臺大出版中心，二○一六。

陳芳妹，《臺南孔廟「萬世師表」御匾——兼論康熙與清初孔廟御匾制度的形成及其傳播》，《故宮學術季刊》，三一卷一期（二○一三），頁一九九－二三○。

陳芳妹，《蔣元樞與臺灣府學的進口禮樂器》，《故宮學術季刊》，三○卷三期（二○一三），頁一二三－一六九。

吳靜芳，〈明嘉靖孔廟祀典改制考析〉，《成大歷史學報》，第三十一號（二○○六），頁一一三－一五二。

郭果六，〈聖、王、賢、儒——漫談孔廟的祭祀體制〉，《故宮文物月刊》，二三卷六期（二○○四），頁九○－一○三。

駱承烈，《孔子歷史地圖集》，北京：中國地圖出版社，二○○三。

孔德懋，《孔府內宅軼事——孔子後裔的回憶》，天津：天津人民出版社，一九八二。

羊春秋，《新譯孔子家語》，臺北：三民書局，一九九六。

謝冰瑩，《新譯四書讀本》，臺北：三民書局，一九八七。

王忠林，《新譯荀子讀本》，臺北：三民書局，二○○九。

許晏駢，《大故事》，臺北：遠景出版社，一九九八。

井上靖，《孔子》，東京：新潮社，一九八九。

錢穆，《孔子傳》，臺北：東大出版社，一九九○。

駱承烈，〈布衣孔子三十而立像〉，《瞭望周刊》，四七期（一九八八），頁三五。

孔德平，〈歷代孔子造像述略〉，《中華文化畫報》，二○○七年第八期。

許瑜翎，《明代孔子「聖蹟圖」研究——以傳世正統九年本《聖蹟圖》為中心》，國立台灣師範大學碩士論文，二○一○。

山東省曲阜市文物管理委員會編，《孔子像‧衍聖公及夫人肖像》，濟南：山東友誼書社，一九八八。

孔子肖像的神話性特徵

此圖孔子已加入「七露」（七孔讓人望見內部）的神性化異表。宋代相書《太清神鑑》記載：「眼睛露，黑白分明不為露；鼻露竅，山根正不為露；口露齒，唇不褰不為露；耳反輪，貼肉生不為露」，是吉人貴相的要素。

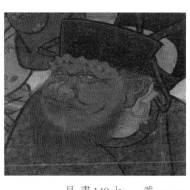

《荀子·非相》記：「仲尼之狀，面如蒙倛。」

上為專文插圖2（頁149）傳《宋蘇漢臣畫五瑞圖》蒙倛面具。

耳—反輪

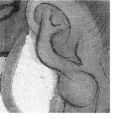

宋代相書《太清神鑑》：「耳反輪，貼肉生不為露。」

《莊子》記老萊子弟子說孔子「末僂而後耳」，亦可釋為耳朵後貼或後反。

眼—露睛或重瞳

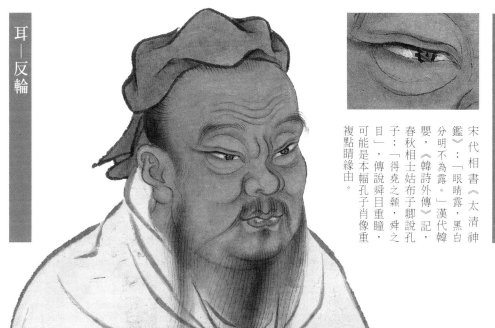

宋代相書《太清神鑑》：「眼睛露，黑白分明不為露。」漢代韓嬰《韓詩外傳》記，春秋相士姑布子卿說孔子：「得堯之顙，舜之目」，傳說舜目重瞳，可能是本幅孔子肖像重複點睛緣由。

口—露齒

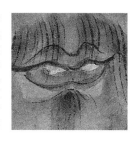

宋代相書《太清神鑑》：「口露齒，唇不褰不為露。」

鼻—露孔

宋代相書《太清神鑑》：「鼻露竅，山根正不為露。」

孔子祖系表

（資料來源：《孔子世家》、〈本姓解第三十九〉。）

人名	世代
帝乙（紂王之父）	十五世祖
微仲衍（紂王異母兄弟，微子之弟）	十四世祖
宋公稽	十三世祖
丁公申	十二世祖
湣公共	十一世祖
弗父何（為宋國公卿）	十世祖
宋父周	九世祖
世子勝	八世祖
正考父	七世祖
孔父嘉（自此以孔為氏）	六世祖
木金父	五世祖
睪夷	四世祖
防叔（避禍奔魯）	曾祖父
伯夏	祖父
叔梁紇	父
孔丘	

168

春秋時代的中國

山戎

赤狄

西戎

薊(北京)
◎

燕
(天津)

鮮虞
(中山) ○

(大原)

汾水

晉

周

秦

渭水

虢
○(西安)

洛陽

泰山▲

(臨淄)

齊

紀

莒

魯

曲阜

衛

沫(朝歌)
◎

滕

郯

宋

泗水

陳

新鄭
◎

鄭

唐

許

息

商丘

萊州
◎

蔡

薛

淮水

庸

鄾

鄧

楚

隋

舒

桐

(武漢)

(南京) ○

吳

吳
(上海)

(杭州) ○

江水

會稽
◎

越

孔子的足跡

萊夷

春秋時代海岸線
現在的海岸線

1. 魯定公十三年（西元前四九七年）春，孔子五十五歲。去魯，西往衛，開始周遊列國，其間曾長留於衛、陳二國。

2. 魯定公十四年（西元前四九六年），孔子五十六歲，去衛，北過匡，因貌似曾攻打匡（今河南省長垣縣西南）地的陽虎，險被匡人拘捕。見《論語·子罕第九》：「子畏於匡。曰：『文王既沒，文不在茲乎？天之將喪斯文也，後死者不得與於斯文也；天之未喪斯文也，匡人其如予何？』」

3. 魯哀公三年（西元前四九二年），孔子六十歲，由衛適曹，再適宋，與弟子習禮大樹下，宋司馬桓魋欲殺之，孔子微服去，適陳。桓魋拔樹洩憤，孔子遂仕於陳。見《史記·孔子世家》：「孔子去曹適宋，與弟子習禮大樹下。宋司馬桓魋欲殺孔子，拔其樹。」《論語·述而第七》：「子曰：『天生德於予，桓魋其如予何？』」

4. 孔子適鄭。見《史記·孔子世家》：「孔子適鄭，與弟子相失，孔子獨立郭東門。鄭人或謂子貢曰：『東門有人，其顙似堯，其項類皋陶，其肩類子產，然自要以下不及禹三寸。累累若喪家之狗。』子貢以實告孔子。孔子欣然笑曰：『形狀，末也。而謂似喪家之狗，然哉！然哉！』」

5. 孔子居陳三歲，為陳湣公識肅慎之矢。魯哀公六年（西元前四八九年），孔子六十三歲，吳伐陳，孔子去陳。絕糧於陳、蔡之間，遂適蔡，見楚葉公。又自葉反陳，自陳反衛。見《論語·公冶長第五》：「子在陳曰：『歸與！歸與！吾黨之小子狂簡，斐然成章，不知所以裁之。』」

6. 魯哀公十一年，（西元前四八四年），孔子六十八歲，魯季康子召孔子，孔子返魯。自其去魯適衛，先後凡十四年，開始晚年教育生活，有若、曾參、言偃、卜商、顓孫師等先後從學。見《論語·子罕第九》：「子曰：『吾自衛反魯，然後樂正，雅頌各得其所。』」

孔子年表（據錢穆（一八九五～一九九〇），《論語新解》整理）

西元紀年	魯國記年	孔子事蹟	重要時事
前七七〇			周平王東遷，東周時代開始。
前七二二	魯隱公元年		春秋時代開始。
前五五一	魯襄公二十二年	一歲　誕生於魯國陬邑。	
前五四九	魯襄公二十四年	三歲　父叔梁紇卒。	
前五三七	魯昭公五年	十五歲　孔子曰後自云：十有五而志於學。	
前五三五	魯昭公七年	十七歲　母顏徵在卒於此年以前。	
前五三三	魯昭公九年	十九歲　娶宋國幷官氏之女為妻。	
前五三二	魯昭公十年	二十歲　得子，因魯君賞賜，取名為鯉，字伯魚。	
前五二五	魯昭公十七年	二十七歲　郯子來朝，孔子見之，學古官名。（其為魯之委吏乘田當在前。）	
前五二二	魯昭公二十年	三十歲　孔子曰後自云：三十而立。孔子初入魯太廟當在前。琴張從遊，當在此時，或稍前。孔子至是始授徒設教。顏無繇、仲由、曾點、冉伯牛、閔損、冉求、仲弓、顏回、高柴、公西赤諸人先後從學。	
前五一八	魯昭公二十四年	三十四歲　孟僖子云：聞將有達者，曰孔丘。遺命其二子孟懿子及南宮敬叔師事孔子學禮。	
前五一七	魯昭公二十五年	三十五歲　孔子適齊，在齊聞《韶》樂。齊景公問政於孔子。	魯三家共攻昭公，昭公奔於齊。
前五一六	魯昭公二十六年	三十六歲　當以是年自齊反。	齊。
前五一五	魯昭公二十七年	三十七歲　吳季箚適齊反，其長子卒，葬嬴、博間，孔子自魯往觀其葬禮。（《閣帖》所收《春秋仲尼延陵帖》即應此事託名而作。）	
前五一三	魯昭公二十九年	三十九歲　《左傳》記孔子是年論晉鑄刑鼎。	
前五一二	魯昭公三十年	四十歲　孔子曰後自云：四十而不惑。	
前五〇五	魯定公五年	四十七歲　魯陽貨執季桓子。陽貨欲見孔子，當在此後。	

西元	魯國紀年	歲	事件	備註
前五〇二	魯定公八年	五十歲	魯三家攻陽貨，陽貨奔陽關。是年，公山弗擾召孔子。孔子曰後自云：五十而知天命。	
前五〇一	魯定公九年	五十一歲	魯陽貨奔齊。孔子始出仕，為魯中都宰。	
前五〇〇	魯定公十年	五十二歲	由中都宰為司空，任司寇，主持齊魯二國夾谷之會。	
前四九八	魯定公十二年	五十四歲	魯聽孔子主張墮三都。墮郈，墮費，又墮成，弗克。孔子因得罪三桓。	
前四九七	魯定公十三年	五十五歲	春，去魯，西往衛，衛人端木賜從遊。周遊列國開始。	
前四九六	魯定公十四年	五十六歲	去衛，北過匡，為匡人誤為陽虎。晉佛肸來召，孔子欲往，不果，重返衛。	
前四九五	魯定公十五年	五十七歲	始見衛靈公，出仕衛，見衛靈公夫人南子。	
前四九四	魯哀公元年	五十八歲	衛靈公問陳，當在今年或明年，孔子遂辭衛仕。	魯哀公即位。
前四九三	魯哀公二年	五十九歲	孔子當在此年前後去衛。	衛靈公卒。
前四九二	魯哀公三年	六十歲	孔子由衛適曹又適宋，宋司馬桓魋欲殺之，孔子微服去，適陳。遂仕於陳。孔子曰後自云：六十而耳順。	
前四八九	魯哀公六年	六十三歲	吳伐陳，孔子去陳。絕糧於陳、蔡之間，遂適蔡，見楚葉公。又自葉反陳，自陳反衛。	
前四八八	魯哀公七年	六十四歲	三度仕衛。	時為衛出公四年。
前四八五	魯哀公十年	六十七歲	妻并官氏卒。	
前四八四	魯哀公十一年	六十八歲	魯季康子召孔子，孔子返魯。自其去魯適衛，先後凡十四年，開始晚年教育生活，有若、曾參、言偃、卜商、顓孫師諸人皆先後從學。	
前四八三	魯哀公十二年	六十九歲	季氏訪田賦事，不答。	
前四八二	魯哀公十三年	七十歲	子孔鯉卒。孔子自云：七十而從心所欲不逾矩。	
前四八一	魯哀公十四年	七十一歲	顏回卒。齊陳恆弒其君，孔子請討之，魯君臣不從，宰予死於此難。孔子《春秋》絕筆。	魯哀公西狩獲麟。
前四八〇	魯哀公十五年	七十二歲	孔子居魯，仲由死於衛。	冬，蒯聵逐其子出公，自立為衛莊公。
前四七九	魯哀公十六年	七十三歲	孔子謝世。魯哀公尊之為「尼父」。	門人廬墓三年，子貢廬墓六年。

歷代封祀孔子相關事蹟與院藏孔子相關書作年表

西元紀年	朝代年號	歷代封諡、奉祀等相關事例	備註
前四七八	魯哀公十七年	魯哀公下令在曲阜闕里孔子舊宅立廟，將孔子生前所居房屋三間改做壽堂，保存陳列孔子生前所用衣、冠、琴、車、書等，並按歲時祭祀。	諸候祭孔之始。
前一九五	漢高祖十二年	漢高祖劉邦命大儒叔孫通據周禮制漢禮，平英布之亂返京，經曲阜孔廟，以太牢祭孔。封孔子九代孫孔騰為「奉祀君」，專主孔子祀事。	此成後世天子太牢祭孔典範。
前四三	漢永光元年	漢元帝召孔子第十三代孫孔霸為帝師，封關內侯，號褒成君，賜食邑八百戶，以稅收按時祭祀孔子。	此開封孔子子孫為侯，以奉祀孔子之例。
一	漢元始元年	漢平帝命孔子第十六代孫孔均世襲褒成侯，追諡孔子為「褒成宣尼公」。	孔子首度封「公」。
五九	漢永平二年	漢明帝詔命祀先師孔子和先聖周公於太學及郡縣學，自此中央政府所在地，與各地方政府學校均舉辦祭孔儀式。	祭孔成為全國性重要活動。
七二	漢永平十五年	漢明帝赴曲阜祭孔，並以七十二弟子從祀。	首以七十二弟子配享。
一五三	漢永興元年	孔子十九世孫孔麟，請依漢代祠廟定制，設立百石卒史，負責孔廟禮器、春秋祭典各項禮儀。	見《乙瑛碑》。
一五六	漢永壽二年	魯相韓敕修整孔廟、置辦禮器，吏民共同捐資立石。	見《禮器碑》。
一六八	漢靈帝建寧元年	魯相史晨祭孔，參與者達九百零七人。	見《史晨後碑》。
一六九	漢靈帝建寧二年	祀孔子，依社稷，出王家穀，春秋行禮。	祭祀孔子規格與社稷神同。見《史晨前碑》。
二二〇	魏黃初元年	封孔子第二十一世孫孔羨為宗聖侯，併奉孔子祀、修孔廟之事。	見《孔羨碑》。
三七二	高句麗小獸林王二年	高句麗設立太學，舉行全國規模祭孔大禮。	韓國祭孔最早相關記載。
四九二	北魏孝文帝太和十六年	魏孝文帝封孔子為「文聖尼父」，祭孔儀典增三獻禮。	
五四一	東魏興和三年	兗州刺史李珽字仲璿，塑孔子及十弟子像，立碑於廟庭。	見《李仲璇修孔子廟碑》。

西元	年號	事件	出處
五八〇	北周大象二年	北周靜帝宇文衍追封孔子為「鄒國公」。	
六一一	隋大業七年	陳宣帝之子陳叔毅，大業年間任官曲阜縣令時重修曲阜孔廟。其時崇儒，大業四年封孔子卅二世孫孔嗣悊為紹聖侯。大業七年事竣，刻石流傳。	見《陳叔毅修孔子廟碑》。
六三〇	唐貞觀四年	詔州、縣學皆立孔子廟。	自此天下多見孔廟。
六三三	唐貞觀七年	唐太宗命虞世南書碑，記唐高祖李淵封孔子二十三世後裔孔德倫為褒聖侯，並修繕孔廟事。	見《虞世南夫子廟堂碑》。
六九〇	武周天授元年	追封孔子為「隆道公」。	
七三九	唐開元二十七年	唐玄宗封孔子為「文宣王」，並分別贈十哲及曾子等共七十七人公、侯、伯爵。	孔子封王之始。
七四〇	唐開元二十八年	詔春秋二仲丁日祭孔時為大祀，舞用八佾。	改往昔「六佾」舞為八佾。
七七三	唐大曆八年	兗州刺史孟休鑒、曲阜縣令裴有象新建曲阜孔廟廟門，刻碑記事，是為《裴孝智撰文宣王廟門記碑》。	見《裴孝智撰文宣王廟門記碑》。
八七〇	唐咸通十一年	孔子卅九世孫孔溫裕奏准出個人薪資修繕整理老舊失修曲阜文宣王廟，事竣後刻石記錄，是為《曲阜文宣王廟記》。	見《曲阜文宣王廟記》。
九六二	宋建隆三年	北宋初年名將王彥超，刻碑記唐末昭宣帝天祐元年（九〇四）將長安舊城「太學并石經」遷至新城事。（碑額「玄聖文宣王」為真宗大中祥符元年（一〇〇八）加謚後刻。）	見《宋建隆三年重修文宣王廟記碑》。
一〇〇八	宋大中祥符元年	宋真宗詔祭孔子廟經史及器用，並封孔子為「玄聖文宣王」。	
一〇〇九	宋大中祥符二年	宋真宗加孔子冕服，桓圭一，冕九旒，服九章，從上公制。追封孔子弟子顏回等十人公爵，曾參等六十二人侯爵，封先儒左丘明等十九人伯爵。同年長安國子監所在永興軍新修玄聖文宣王廟大門。	見《永興軍新修玄聖文宣王廟大門記碑》。
一〇一二	大中祥符五年	宋真宗為孔子改號為「至聖」文宣王。並詔進封配享諸子。	見《宋真宗御製至聖文宣王贊碑》。
一〇五五	宋至和二年	封孔子四十七代孫孔宗願為「衍聖公」，並令孔門嫡長子世襲之。	
一一〇四	宋崇寧三年	詔易七十二子以周之冕服，詔名文宣王殿曰「大成」。	「大成殿」之始。
一一〇五	宋崇寧四年	增文宣王廟像冕十二旒，衮服九章，又頒祭服制度於州縣，令皆以法服行禮。	天子用十二旒十二章。
一一〇九	宋大觀三年	釋奠樂成。樂章各有詞曲。	

西元紀年	朝代年號	歷代封諡、奉祀等相關事例	備註
一一一〇	宋大觀四年	文宣王廟像改執鎮圭，廟門增立二十四戟，並如王者之制。	北宋天子宮殿與宗廟立戟二十四。
一一一六	宋政和六年	賜孔廟樂器、禮器各一副，頒釋奠樂章於闕里。	
一一四六	西夏仁宗三年	夏人慶三年（紹興十六年）三月，西夏仁宗頒布詔令：「尊孔子為文宣帝，令州郡悉立廟祀，殿庭宏敞，並如帝制。」…八月，策舉人。立唱名法，復設童子科。	西夏予孔子皇帝名分，殿庭規格均與西夏皇帝同。
一二六七	元至元四年	元世祖敕上都重建孔廟。	
一三〇八	元至大元年	封孔子「大成至聖文宣王」。	元武宗之姊魯國大長公主祥哥喇吉參與祭孔，為史上女性祭孔第一人。
一三六八	明洪武元年	置林廟洒掃戶一百一十五戶。	
一三七一	明洪武四年	定於每年仲春二月仲秋八月上旬丁日，拂曉釋奠祭孔。賜祭田兩千大頃，更定孔廟祭器樂舞。改籩豆八為十；祭器由木易以瓷。	
一四七六	明成化十二年	祭酒周洪謨請增孔廟禮樂。定籩豆十二。	
一四九六	明弘治九年	增祭孔樂舞生二十六人，與天子樂舞七十二人相等。	
一五三〇	明嘉靖九年	更定孔廟祀典，封「至聖先師」。	
一六三三	寬永九年	日本儒學家林羅山於上野國忍岡興建先聖殿，供奉孔子及顏子、曾子、子思、孟子。	日本供奉孔子之始。
一六四五	清順治二年	封「大成至聖文宣先師」。	
一六五七	清順治十四年	改諡「至聖先師」。	
一六八四	清康熙二十三年	清聖祖至闕里祀孔子，行三跪九叩禮，賜御書「萬世師表」匾。	
一七二五	清雍正三年	令天下「丘」姓者避孔子諱，寫作「邱」。	
一七二九	清雍正七年	頒內府新制大成殿祭器、鎮圭、曲柄寶蓋及二十四戟。	
一七三〇	清雍正八年	孔廟大成殿塑像落成，詔設聖廟執事官四十員。	
一七四八	清乾隆十三年	清高宗至闕里祀孔子，後多次至闕里釋奠孔子。	
一七七一	清乾隆三十六年	諭頒周範銅器於孔廟。	
一九〇六	清光緒三十二年	學部頒布尊孔為全國教育宗旨之一。	

院藏孔子相關書法時代序列

淳化閣法帖　魯司寇孔丘延陵帖

又名〈春秋仲尼延陵帖〉，亦見於《宋拓大觀帖》、《明拓寶賢堂集古法帖冊》、《清乾隆御製重刻淳化閣帖等》。全文為「烏呼。延陵封邑有吳君子之墓。」據清人王澍（一六六八－一七四三）考證，世傳以此為孔子替史稱「延陵季子」的春秋時代吳國賢人季劄墓碑書篆之作，然篆法敦古，疑為漢代以前之人託名題墓。北宋淳化中為閣帖收入，亦為縮臨小字本。

西漢五鳳二年（西元前五六）刻石

又名「漢魯孝王刻石」，金章宗明昌二年（一一九一）重修曲阜孔廟時，自魯靈光殿址西南釣魚池石塊中發現，現置曲阜孔廟。共十三字：「五鳳二年（西元前五六）、魯卅四年六月四日成。」西漢隸書至今少見，此為西漢最有名的刻石之一，結體不算方整，也無明顯波勢，字體上承秦隸，篆意較濃，至為古拙樸厚。其中「年」字豎筆向下延伸極長，與出土同期漢簡同趣。

東漢永興元年（一五三）乙瑛碑

詳前展品說明。

東漢永興二年（一五四）孔謙碣

又名〈孔謙殘碑〉、〈孔德讓碑〉。東漢永興二年（一五四）刻。原在孔林，清初移入孔廟，現存東廡。碑圓首，有穿，無額無題。文共八行，每行十字，碑文隸書。字體波磔較長，雖磨損嚴重，仍能窺見其字體莊重雍容的淳厚風格。孔謙，字德讓，曾官郡曹史，孔子二十代孫，孔宙之子，孔晨、孔褒（一作孔曜、字文禮）、孔融（字文舉）、孔昱（字世元）等為兄弟。

東漢永壽元年（一五五）孔君碑並跋

又名〈孔君墓碣〉、〈孔少垂墓碑〉，東漢永壽元年（一五五）刻。圓首，額陰刻「孔君之墓」四篆字。文隸書八行，行十五字，大多殘缺漫漶，勉強可讀得所刻年月及孔君官職等五十二字，由官職僅知此為孔子十九世孫孔少垂墓碣。清乾隆五十八年（一七九三）發現於孔子墓圍牆外，移入孔廟，現藏於山東曲阜。隸法淳厚蒼勁，可供取法。此拓本右下角附翁方綱（一七三三－一八一八）題記。

東漢永壽二年（一五六）漢禮器碑

詳前展品說明。

東漢延熹七年（一六四）泰山都尉孔宙碑

東漢桓帝延熹七年（一六四）造，為孔子十九世孫孔宙墓碑文。孔宙為孔融之父，《後漢書》有傳，他於泰山都尉任內，正竭力平定匪亂，卻因病辭官，延禧六年卒。門生為立此碑，以表彰他的功德。碑今在曲阜孔廟。本碑以圓轉的篆書筆法寫隸，書法流麗華美，柔中帶剛，字體特別橫長，呈現擺蕩的動感，顯得宏博寬大、風度翩翩。

東漢建寧元年（一六八）漢史晨碑

詳前展品說明。

漢豫州從事孔褒碑殘碑

又名《孔褒碑》，隸書額題：「漢故豫州從事孔君之碑」。無立碑年月，清雍正三年（一七二五）鄉民犂田時出土，隨即移入曲阜孔廟。碑文隸書，書體嚴整，書風蒼厚。字共十四行，滿行三十字。剝蝕嚴重，第十三、十四行全毀，拓本多為十二行本。孔褒（一作孔曜），字文禮（？－一六九），東漢人。於孔宙七子中行三，孔融之兄，舉孝廉、辟豫州從事。

東漢建寧四年（一七一）漢孔彪碑

東漢建寧四年（一七一）立，全名《漢故博陵太守孔府君碑》，原石存曲阜孔廟。碑主人孔彪，字元上，孔子十九世孫，孔宙之弟，孔融之叔。歷官郎中、尚書侍郎、博陵太守等。年少好學，以德行受知鄉裡，尤以博陵太守任內政績卓著。故屬崔烈等感懷其德，立碑稱頌。碑文隸書，筆畫精勁，結構謹嚴，向列漢隸名品之一。惜剝蝕較甚，損字較多。

漢魯相謁孔廟殘碑

又名《孔宏殘碑》，《吉日令晨碑》，碑現存山東曲阜。立碑年月不明，碑文結體方整豐肥，寬博厚重，神采甚似漢熹平二年（一七三）《魯峻碑》。碑字漫漶，多不可讀，乾隆五十四年（一七八九）錢塘藏書及金石學家何元錫（一七六六－一八二九，字夢華）洗石精拓本，可辨字

較多，碑陰亦以何氏拓本字多可見，題字亦較清晰。

東漢熹平四年（一七五）石經春秋殘石墨拓本

中國史上最早的官定本儒家教科書，又稱「漢石經」。東漢靈帝熹平四年（一七五）學界領袖及書法家蔡邕以經籍去聖久遠，俗儒穿鑿，疑誤後學，奏准正定《六經》文字。邕乃自書丹於碑，使工鐫刻立於太學門外。竣工於光和六年（一八三）。以隸書一體刻《魯詩》、《周易》、《尚書》、《儀禮》、《春秋》、《公羊傳》及《論語》七經，共四十六石。及碑始立，觀視摹寫者，車乘日千餘輛，填塞街陌。

魏黃初元年（二二〇）孔羨碑

詳前展品說明。

魏正始二年（二四一）三體石經墨拓本

為增刊古文經以補《熹平石經》獨用今文經之不足，三國曹魏正始二年（二四一），於魏都洛陽南郊太學講堂西側刻立《正始石經》。以古文、小篆與隸書刻《尚書》、《春秋》、《左傳》，凡三十五石，人稱「三體石經」或「正始石經」。北朝以來，屢遭毀損，現存殘石多塊，古文部分保存了不少相對原始的古文字形體，篆法精妙，成為研究中國古文字學與書法的珍貴資料。

東魏興和三年（五四一）李仲璇修孔子廟碑

詳前展品說明。

隋大業七年（六一一）陳叔毅修孔子廟碑

〈修孔子廟碑〉或名〈陳叔毅修孔子廟碑〉，碑文隸書，篆額，原石現存於山東曲阜孔廟。陳叔毅，字子嚴，穎川許昌人，為陳宣帝之子，大業年間任官曲阜縣令時，重修曲阜孔廟。大業七年事竣，濟州秀才仲孝俊撰文記其始末，刻石流傳。其時尊崇儒教，先於大業四年，封孔子卅二世孫孔嗣悊為紹聖侯，故碑文有云：「新開紹聖，重光闕裡。」碑文隸法清峻，結體略近方整，惜未詳具書者為何人。

唐貞觀七年（六三三）虞世南夫子廟堂碑

記載唐高祖封孔子二十三世後裔孔德倫為褒聖侯，並修繕孔廟事。碑文為初唐著名書法家虞世南（五五八～六三八）六十九歲時寫，書風淳熟，筆法圓勁秀朗，平實端莊，筆勢舒展，用筆含蓄樸素，一派平和雅潤氣象，是初唐碑刻傑作與歷代公認的虞書妙品。此碑刻成不久火毀，武周長安三年（七〇三）重刻又毀，唐拓本今已罕見。本院藏本闕字與清人王澍所校明內庫宋本略同。似宋代王彥超摹刻本，因石在西安，謂之「西廟堂碑」。

清三希堂法帖　唐歐陽詢卜商帖

又稱〈卜商讀書帖〉，今有曾入北宋內府之唐人雙鉤廓填本藏於北京故宮。帖共五十三字，筆力峭勁，行氣淹貫，字畫飽滿豐腴，起筆簡捷而少婉約之勢，點畫起止強調方切硬折，鋒銳如斬釘截鐵。此文記子夏答

孔子問《尚書》讀後感事，出自《尚書大傳》，並見於歐陽詢所撰《藝文類聚》卷五十五〈雜文部・讀書〉，可能是歐陽詢手稿片段。

祕閣帖　唐歐陽詢夢奠帖

全稱〈仲尼夢奠帖〉，紙本墨蹟曾入南宋內府，現藏於遼寧省博物館。帖共七十八字無款印，書法筆力蒼勁古茂，轉折自如，上下脈絡映帶清晰，結構穩重沉實，運筆從容，氣韻流暢，筆力險勁，嫵媚而剛勁，為初唐書法家歐陽詢（五五七～六四一）晚年所書，清勁絕塵。所言事見《史記・孔子世家》，孔子死前七日「夢坐奠於兩楹之間」，是其祖殷人殯葬之禮，預知自己將死。

唐開元十一年（七二三）孔子顏子讚殘石
宋夏鰭孔廟題名

唐開元十一年（七二三）刻，碑文楷書，左刻唐睿宗太極元年（七一二）撰孔子讚，右刻唐玄宗開元八年（七二〇）撰顏子讚。碑右側及下部已殘，今存全石左上角，僅有讚詩而無讚題、作者。石上被鑿多條橫線，造成多字殘損。同石碑陰有北宋政和丙申六年（一一一六）夏鰭拜祠題記，但南宋孔傳《東家雜記》和金末孔元措《孔氏族庭廣記》所列唐代碑目均無此碑。

唐天寶元年（七四二）兗公之頌碑

兗公即孔子第一高徒，德行之首顏回（前五二一年～前四八一年），唐玄宗開元年間追封「兗公」。碑文中為避唐高祖諱，將顏回之字子淵改

為子泉。根據碑文，都督李庭誨以孔子（宣王）已有銘記，而兗公卻無頌為由，命曲阜縣令張之宏作文，包文該書寫，天寶元年（七四二）建碑。碑額隸書。明代以前此碑下半部曾埋於土中，故舊拓每行皆有一二字缺損，原碑現存於山東曲阜孔廟內。

唐大曆八年（七七三）裴孝智撰文宣王廟門記
詳前展品說明。

唐開成二年（八三七）石經儀禮碑墨拓本購拓

又稱唐石經，文宗大和七年（八三四）始刻，開成二年（八三七）完成。以唐代標準楷書刻《周易》等儒家經書十二種，共一百一十四石，每石兩面刻字，共逾六十五萬字。北宋年間數次遷置《開成石經》，最後移至府學北墉，即今西安碑林，是中國古代保存最完好的儒家刻經。此拓為《儀禮》第一至十七卷部分。

唐咸通十一年（八七〇）曲阜文宣王廟記

文宣王廟即指孔廟，因唐開元廿七年（七三九），追諡孔子為文宣王，以示尊崇。咸通年間，由於農作欠收經年，曲阜文宣王廟老舊失修，孔子卅九世孫孔溫裕有心復其舊觀，奏准出個人薪資加以修繕整理。事竣後賈防撰文記其經過，附及孔溫裕蒙獲嘉獎始末，刻石流傳，原石現存於山東曲阜孔廟。碑文及碑額均作楷書，筆畫瘦勁，有柳公權書法之清朗風貌，可以略窺晚唐楷書的趨向。

北宋建隆三年（九六二）重修文宣王廟記碑墨拓本
詳前展品說明。

北宋太平興國七年（九八二）夢英書唐程浩撰夫子廟堂記碑墨拓本

釋夢英，北宋僧人，號宣義、臥雲叟、南嶽衡州（湖南）人。嫻通《華嚴經》，宋太宗曾召賜紫服。篆書承繼李陽冰傳統，尤工玉箸篆，以瘦硬著稱。本幅為宋太宗太平興國七年（九八二）刻《宋釋夢英十八體書碑》碑陰，記年為宋太祖乾德五年（九六七），夢英以楷字重書唐代宗大曆二年（七六七），駕部郎中程浩為陝西扶風縣文宣王廟所撰「夫子廟堂記」，文載於《唐文粹》，原碑顏真卿楷書碑文，徐浩題額。

北宋崇寧二年（一一〇三）米芾孔子手植檜贊

宋崇寧二年（一一〇三）刻。碑圓首，行草刻文六行，宋代著名書畫家米芾（一〇五一—一一〇七）撰並書，米書行草得力于王獻之（三四一—三八六），用筆俊邁，有「風檣陣馬，沉著痛快」之評。此碑運筆瀟灑俊逸，神采飛揚，筋骨雄毅，剛健端莊，體現了米芾行草的特點，可惜多次被火，殘損嚴重。原碑位於孔子手植檜側，後移入十三碑亭院內及孔廟東廡，現存漢魏碑刻陳列館。

北宋大中祥符二年（一〇〇九）永興軍新修玄聖文宣王廟大門記碑墨拓本

宋永興軍新修玄聖文宣王廟大門記，北宋真宗大中祥符二年（一〇〇九）六月立碑，碑文楷書，共二十二行，行四十四字。孫僅撰文，冉宗閔書，張格篆額，安文璨刻字，今存西安碑林，已裂為二石。永興軍為長安國子監所在，新修玄聖文宣王廟大門，刻碑記事。碑額「玄聖文宣王」為大中祥符元年加孔子冕服，桓圭一，冕九旒，服九章，從上公制時所封。碑文「奉祀典順考禮文因開元之舊封，增玄聖之新號」即此。

北宋大中祥符五年（一〇一二）宋真宗御製玄聖文宣王贊碑墨拓本

宋御製玄聖文宣王贊並加號詔，宋真宗（九六八－一〇二二）撰，王嗣宗書，宋大中祥符五年（一〇一二）刻，碑額篆書，內容敘述在唐開元廿七年追諡孔子為「文宣王」後，北宋大中祥符年間宋真宗趙恆（九六八－一〇二二）駕幸曲阜，又為孔子加號「玄聖」。並且詔進封配享諸子。王嗣宗（九四四－一〇二二）汾州（今山西汾陽）人，字希阮。宋太祖開寶八年（九七五）狀元，歷事三朝，官至樞密副使、檢校太尉。喜寫文章，書箚尤甚。

北宋天聖八年（一〇三〇）孔勖祖廟祝文

孔勖，字自牧，孔子四十三代孫中興祖孔仁玉（九一二－九五六）第四子。進士及第，宋真宗東封泰山，躬詣孔廟，召孔勖對，授太常博士、知曲阜縣，以工部侍郎致仕。此碑為宋真宗天聖八年（一〇三〇）孔子第四十四代孫孔勖祭祀祖廟祝禱奉告之文，祖廟即孔廟。撰文者孔道輔（九八五－一〇三九）為其長子。碑文楷書，書者孔彥輔，為孔勖第三子。

北宋景祐二年（一〇三五）孔道輔祖廟祭文

孔道輔（九八五－一〇三九），孔子第四十五代孫，字原魯，初名延魯，宋史有傳。大中祥符五年（一〇一二）進士，九年（一〇一六）遷大理寺丞，知仙源縣（今曲阜），主持孔子祀事。此碑為宋真宗景祐二年（一〇三五）孔道輔以孔子後裔身分致祭之文，碑文楷書，書者張宗益，為孔道輔之父孔勖門人，神宗時以尚書工部郎中知相州致仕。

Contents

Essay

The Forms of Confucius in Painting and Confucian Themes in Calligraphy

Preface

Confucius is venerated as the "Sage for All Time," meaning his ideas are considered applicable to every age. Now in the 21st century, with the quickening pace of globalization and modernization, the learning and conduct of Confucius continue to stand the test of time. Not only that, the ideas of Confucius have been able to break down barriers of time and space to emerge as a trend that even Western culture willingly accepts.

Taiwan, in particular, has long been blessed as a recipient of Confucian thought. Nowadays, this includes the familiar children's primer of *The Three Character Classic, Standards for Students* becoming more popular in recent years and even recited in Taiwanese, and *The Analects of Confucius* as a basic teaching material for Chinese culture in senior high schools. All of these facets represent the crystallization of Confucian ideals. As a result, even today, the heritage of Confucian values continues to exert a major influence on contemporary society, especially Confucian cultural circles in East Asia.

Confucius, regarded as one of the greatest educators in Chinese history, is known as the "Teacher Exemplar for a Myriad Generations." His cultural values transmitted over the years appear in his humanistic spirit and educational ideals. More than two millennia ago, it was Confucius who advocated that "education is for everyone, irrespective of social background" and that "different teaching methods apply to different students," ideas which greatly expanded the range and scope of education and reverberate today. In fact, this popularization of education continues to serve as one of the greatest foundations of and inspirations for contemporary society.

Museums, as institutions open to and for the general public, also hope that people can use and become a part of them as important sites for social education. The National Palace Museum collection, a participant in the long course of history, has been a filter for the cultural heritage of painting and calligraphy passed down through the ages, naturally preserving a large number of works related to Confucius. The confluence of the museum as a site for education and history can help reinvigorate the legacy of Confucian thought from the past, which is precisely one of the goals of this exhibition.

The organization of this exhibit on "Teacher Exemplar for a Myriad Generations: Confucius in Painting, Calligraphy, and Print Through the Ages" is an attempt to avoid the stereotypical impression of Confucian sayings as didactic and disciplinarian in nature. Rather, the perspective of visual imagery here shows us other aspects from the life of Confucius, such as playing music. There are also stories related to Confucius, including his admiration for the bravery of Bian Zhuangzi in killing a tiger, or those about his disciples. In terms of calligraphy, steles familiar to contemporary students of calligraphy, such as "Yi Ying," "Ritual Vessels," and "Shi Chen," all commemorate him or record repairs to the Temple of Confucius. These stone engravings and stele rubbings that have survived and circulated continue to serve as important models of calligraphy. The National Palace Museum thus sincerely hopes this exhibition will be an invitation to and reminder for the general public to reexamine the life and ideas of Confucius one more time through painting, calligraphy, and prints so as to acquire a new inspiration for and sources of learning in today's ever-changing society.

Jeng-yi LIN
Director, National Palace Museum

Introduction

In 1684, early during the Qing dynasty, the Kangxi emperor embarked on his first southern inspection tour and one his stops was Qufu, the hometown of Confucius (551-449 BCE), the most celebrated teacher and philosopher in Chinese history. While there, Kangxi presented a plaque in his own writing with "Teacher Exemplar for a Myriad Generations," which was hung in the Hall of Great Achievement at the Temple of Confucius. In the following year, the court ordered that rubbing copies be made of the plaque and presented to all temples in the country dedicated to Confucius. Thereafter, "Teacher Exemplar for a Myriad Generations" would become synonymous with Confucius. Today, the plaque for "Teacher Exemplar for a Myriad Generations" hanging at the Hall of Great Achievement in Tainan's Temple of Confucius, the earliest one in Taiwan, is also its largest.

The ancestors of Confucius descended from kings of the late Shang dynasty through nobility in the Song state, but Confucius himself was born in Lu. In Chinese, his surname is Kong (from the family name Zi), personal name Qiu, and style name Zhongni, with later generations referring to him as Kongzi ("Master Kong") or Kongfuzi ("Grand Master Kong"), from which his Latinized name derives. A philosopher and educator who lived during the Eastern Zhou dynasty, Confucius was an important scholar as well. He edited *The Book of Poetry* and *The Book of Documents*, added commentaries to *The I Ching*, established official rites and music, and compiled *The Spring and Autumn Annals*, having a hand in many of the classics that would become required reading among later generations preparing for the civil service examinations. As a result, Confucius came to exert an enormous influence in Chinese culture. And people even in Japan, Korea, Vietnam, and Southeast Asia were impacted by his teachings, forming a sphere of Confucian culture.

Mencius, the most famous Confucian after Confucius himself, once referred to the master as a "Sage for All Time," meaning that the philosophy of Confucius applies to all times. The sayings, events, and travels to various states of Confucius are preserved in *The Analects of Confucius* and *The School Sayings of Confucius*, being scattered in *Records of the Grand Historian* and the writings of various philosophers as well. The collection of the National Palace Museum is fortunate to have many works related to Confucius. In addition to images of Confucius in paintings and illustrated woodblock prints, there are also many calligraphic works, including famous examples in Han clerical script, rubbings of steles over the ages, classic sayings, and plaques from the imperial brush, all serving as historical traces of the veneration for Confucianism since the Han dynasty. This special exhibition features 35 works divided into four sections: "Portraits of the Sage," "Calligraphy on Confucius," "Confucians Through the Ages," and "Illustrating the Classics." Together, they are offered with respect to the legacy of Confucius, "Teacher Exemplar for a Myriad Generations," whose sagacious virtue has nurtured Chinese culture for ages and will continue to do so for years to come.

Descriptions of the Plates

I. Portraits of the Sage

Although Confucius in his later years had become a teacher to those in power, the earliest record of an image in his likeness does not appear until "Biography of Cai Yong" in *Book of the Later Han*. In 178 CE, the School at the Gate of the Great Capital was established with images of Confucius and his 72 disciples painted on the walls, representing a gap of more than six centuries since Confucius had passed away. The various representations of Confucius seen today form the picture that we have of him, and most come from later attempts to portray him from literary descriptions and the imagination.

1.
Half Portraits of the Great Sage and Virtuous Men of Old: Confucius

Anonymous, Yuan dynasty (1279-1368)
Album leaf, ink and colors on paper, 33.3 x 24.3 cm

This album of sixty leaves begins with a portrait of Confucius and ends with that of Xu Heng (1209-1281), spanning the Spring and Autumn period (770-476 BCE) up to the Yuan dynasty and including 120 notable Confucians. The album was originally stored in the Nanxun Palace, where portraits of rulers and sages over the ages were stored at the Qing dynasty (1644-1911) court. Judging from the names in the title labels in the upper right corners of the portraits, the album must have been done after the Yuan dynasty court ennobled Confucius' major disciples in 1330.

On display in this exhibition are the first seven leaves in order featuring Confucius' Four Attendants and the Ten Philosophers, who are seen in "Book 11, Those of Preceding Eras" from *The Analects of Confucius*. In it, Confucius cites four disciples most notable for their conduct: Yan Yuan, Min Ziqian, Ran Boniu, and Zonggong. For their speech, there are Zai Wo and Zigong. For their administration, they are Ran You and Jilu. And for their literary skills, there are Ziyou and Zixia. The arrangement of the Four Attendants was established in 1267, late in the Southern Song period, and comprised Yan Yuan, Zeng Shen, Kong Ji, and Meng Ke.

2.
Half Portraits of the Great Sage and Virtuous Men of Old: Yan Hui

Anonymous, Yuan dynasty (1279-1368)
Album leaf, ink and colors on paper, 33.3 x 24.3 cm

Yan Hui (521-481 BCE), a native of Lu with the style name Ziyuan and known as Yanzi and Yan Yuan, was thirty years younger than Confucius. A diligent man of few words, he did not anger easily or make the same mistake twice. Leading a simple life and taking joy in the Way, he is ranked first among the "Ten Philosophers" of Confucius in terms of virtue and considered the disciple of whom Confucius thought most highly. He unfortunately passed away at the age of 41, much to the grief of Confucius. In the Zhengshi second year of the Wei in the Three Kingdoms period (241 CE), Emperor Shaodi ordered "Yan Yuan as an Attendant," making him the earliest of Confucius' disciples to be enshrined with him. In the Kaiyuan 27th year of the Tang emperor Xuanzong (739), he was ennobled as the "Duke of Yan" and further ennobled in the Zhishun first year of the Yuan emperor Wenzong (1330) as "Duke of the State of Yan, Reviving the Sage."

3.

Half Portraits of the Great Sage and Virtuous Men of Old: Zeng Shen

Anonymous, Yuan dynasty (1279-1368)
Album leaf, ink and colors on paper, 33.3 x 24.3 cm

Zeng Shen (505-435 BCE), from Wucheng in the state of Lu (modern Bixian, Shandong), had the style name Ziyu and was referred to by later generations as Zengzi. He was 46 years younger than Confucius, his father also a disciple of Confucius. Zeng Shen was famous for his filial piety and summarized the Way of Confucius in two words: "benevolence" and "loyalty." He also proposed the method of personal cultivation known as "I daily examine myself on three points." He was the teacher of Confucius' grandson, Kong Ji. Starting from the Zongzhang first year of the Tang emperor Gaozong (668), he was ennobled and posthumously appointed as "Junior Protector of the Heir Apparent." In the Xianchun third year of the Southern Song emperor Duzong (1267), he was elevated to the rank of "Attendant" to Confucius and ennobled as "Duke of Cheng, Revering the Sage" in the Zhishun first year of the Yuan emperor Wenzong (1330).

4.

Half Portraits of the Great Sage and Virtuous Men of Old: Kong Ji

Anonymous, Yuan dynasty (1279-1368)
Album leaf, ink and colors on paper, 33.3 x 24.3 cm

Kong Ji (483-402 BCE), Confucius' grandson, had the style name Zisi and was known as "Shusheng," or "Summarizing the Sage." The son of Kong Li (532-483 BCE), he once was a student of Zeng Shen, and his disciple reportedly was the teacher of Mencius. The author of *Master Zisi*, his only work to survive is *Doctrine of the Mean*, which advocates maintaining neutrality and avoiding extremes in the pursuit of "sincerity" as a form of personal cultivation. Kong Ji was ennobled by Emperor Huizong in the Song dynasty as "Marquis of Yishui" and then by the Yuan emperor Wenzong as "Duke of the State of Yi, Continuing the Sage." Along with Yan Hui as "Reviving the Sage," Zeng Shen as "Revering the Sage," and Mencius as "The Second Sage," they became known as the Four Attendants.

5.

Half Portraits of the Great Sage and Virtuous Men of Old: Meng Ke

Anonymous, Yuan dynasty (1279-1368)
Album leaf, ink and colors on paper, 33.3 x 24.3 cm

Meng Ke (372-289 BCE), also known as Mengzi (and romanized as Mencius), was a native of the state of Zou (modern Zoucheng in Shandong) and a representative of Confucianism in the Warring States period. His ideas mainly deal with the nature of goodness and the political ideals of humanism and righteousness. Starting in the Tang dynasty with Han Yu (768-824), who wrote "Seeking the Origin of the Way," Mencius has been considered the only true successor to the orthodoxy of Confucius in the pre-Qin era, his status coming to surpass even that of Yan Hui. In 1071, during the Northern Song dynasty, Emperor Shenzong for the first time included *Mencius* as one of the classics for the civil service examinations. Then, in 1083, Mencius was ennobled as the "Duke of Zou" and in the following year approved for veneration as an Attendant in the Temple of Confucius. In the Southern Song, *Mencius* was included as one of the Four Books and actually ranked higher than the Five Classics.

6.

Half Portraits of the Great Sage and Virtuous Men of Old: Min Sun

Anonymous, Yuan dynasty (1279-1368)
Album leaf, ink and colors on paper, 33.3 x 24.3 cm

Min Sun (536-487 BCE), a native of Lu, had the style name Ziqian. One of the "Ten Philosophers" among Confucius' disciples, Min was fifteen years his younger and known for his virtue and cultivation. Confucius once remarked about him: "The man talks not much but speaks to the point," showing him to be a person of few words and steadiness. Confucius also praised him as "Filial to the point where no one can come between him and his parents or siblings." He is also the subject of "Flimsy Clothes But Obedient to Mother" in *Twenty-four Exemplars of Filial Piety*, in which he was given poor winter clothing by his stepmother but still treated her respectfully. In "Book 6, Yong Ye" from *The Analects of Confucius*, Min Sun shows displeasure with the arrogance of the Ji ruler and quits his post of Minister of Bi. Later emperors, however, would ennoble Min Sun in Bi, such as "Marquis of Bi" in the Tang dynasty and "Duke of Bi" in the Song dynasty, apparently to indicate that the usurpation by Ji was no longer an issue at that time.

7.

Half Portraits of the Great Sage and Virtuous Men of Old: Ran Geng

Anonymous, Yuan dynasty (1279-1368)
Album leaf, ink and colors on paper, 33.3 x 24.3 cm

Ran Geng (544-? BCE), a native of Lu with the style name Boniu, belonged to the same clan as Ran Yong. One of the Ten Philosophers, Ran Geng was seven years younger than Confucius. Passing away at a young age from an infectious disease, his year of death is unknown. Respected for his virtuous conduct, when Confucius was serving as a judge, Ran Geng was the Minister of Zhongdu. Few records survive of Ran, but the Four Attendants and Ten Philosophers of Confucius come from "Book 11, Those of Preceding Eras" in *The Analects of Confucius*, which states: "The Master said, 'Of those who followed me in Chen and Cai, none are at my door now.' Of virtuous conduct are Yan Yuan, Min Ziqian, Ran Boniu, and Zhonggong; in speech, Zai Wo and Zigong; in governing, Ran You and Jilu; in literary studies, Ziyou and Zixia." Ran Geng was one of the disciples who accompanied Confucius in his period of wandering.

8.

Half Portraits of the Great Sage and Virtuous Men of Old: Ran Yong

Anonymous, Yuan dynasty (1279-1368)
Album leaf, ink and colors on paper, 33.3 x 24.3 cm

Ran Yong (522-? BCE), a native of Lu with the style name Zhonggong, was 29 years younger than Confucius. In the Tang dynasty, he was ennobled as the "Marquis of Xue" and in the Song dynasty as the "Duke of Xiapi," which was changed to the "Duke of Xue." Born to a lowly father, he nonetheless became a man of great sincerity and integrity with a magnanimous character. Known for his virtuous conduct, he was also skilled at governing. In 482 BCE, the third year after returning to Lu with Confucius from his travels to various states, Ran Yong served the ruler Ji Huanzi (?-492 BCE), becoming a minister for the Ji clan at the age of 41. In *The Analects of Confucius*, Ran Yong is seen asking Confucius several times about governing and benevolence, Confucius praising him as a man worthy of "facing south," or being a ruler, possessing both character and skill in governing.

9.

Half Portraits of the Great Sage and Virtuous Men of Old: Zai Yu

Anonymous, Yuan dynasty (1279-1368)
Album leaf, ink and colors on paper, 33.3 x 24.3 cm

Zai Yu (522-458 BCE), a native of Lu who had the style name Ziwo and was also called Zai Wo, was one of the Ten Philosophers. Younger than Confucius by 29 years and known for his skill in speech, he is the student in *The Analects of Confucius* most admonished by Confucius for his startling comments. He is known for his tendency to sleep during the day and for proposing that the period of mourning for the death of a parent be shortened from three years to one, which Confucius criticized as being heartless. Mencius, however, claimed that Zai Yu highly admired Confucius and was someone who "had the wisdom to know the sage." Perhaps because of his intellectual curiosity and confidence, he often proposed ideas that differed from those of Confucius, which is probably why the editors of *The Analects of Confucius* were left with the above impression of him.

10.

Half Portraits of the Great Sage and Virtuous Men of Old: Duanmu Ci

Anonymous, Yuan dynasty (1279-1368)
Album leaf, ink and colors on paper, 33.3 x 24.3 cm

Duanmu Ci (520-446 BCE), a native of Wei with the style name Zigong, was 31 years younger than Confucius and known for his gift of speech. He was a favored disciple of Confucius, who called him "a person of high caliber." Skilled in the art of debate and a man of great talent, he went on to serve as a minister in both the states of Lu and Wei, advocating a system of teaching in Wu based on that of Lu, and becoming known for his achievements in diplomacy. He was also a gifted businessman, becoming the wealthiest of all Confucius' disciples. After Confucius passed away, Duanmu Ci built a hut by his grave and mourned for three years and then three years more to accompany his master. Also dedicating himself to propagating the teachings of Confucius, records about Duanmu Ci in *The Analects of Confucius* suggest that he was one of the main forces behind its compilation.

11.

Half Portraits of the Great Sage and Virtuous Men of Old: Ran Qiu

Anonymous, Yuan dynasty (1279-1368)
Album leaf, ink and colors on paper, 33.3 x 24.3 cm

Ran Qiu (522-? BCE), a native of Lu known by the style name Ziyou and also called Ran You, was 29 years younger than Confucius. In "Xian Asks" from *The Analects of Confucius*, Confucius replied to a question posed by Zilu about what constitutes a complete person, referring in his answer to the art of Ran Qiu, the wisdom of Cang Wuzhong, the self-denial of Meng Gongzhuo, and the bravery of Bian Zhuangzi. Ran Qiu was man of humility and many talents also renowned for his skill in governing. He served as the family minister for Ji Kangzi (?-468 BCE) and supported Confucius in returning to the state of Lu in his late years. However, he was condemned for levying duties and taxes on behalf of the Ji clan and being unable to prevent it from usurping the royal privilege to conduct rites at Mount Tai. Ran Qiu's situation reflected the indirect political influence of Confucius.

12.

Half Portraits of the Great Sage and Virtuous Men of Old: Zhong You

Anonymous, Yuan dynasty (1279-1368)
Album leaf, ink and colors on paper, 33.3 x 24.3 cm

Zhong You (542-480 BCE), from the city of Bian in Lu with the style name Zilu and also known as Jilu, was nine years younger than Confucius and the disciple who spent the longest time with him. In addition to studying poetry and the rites, Zhong You also was the coachman for Confucius and helped guard him during his sojourn from state to state. Rash and straightforward by nature, Zhong You was known for his courage and strength, keeping his word, and being loyal and steadfast in his duties. Filial in performing duties for his parents, he is the main character in one of the *Twenty-four Exemplars of Filial Piety*, in which he contents himself with meager greens but is willing to carry rice over long distances for his parents. Zhong You was gifted at governing and first served in Lu, later taking office in Wei. He became a minister for the Ji clan and later an official for Kong Kui of Wei, dying as he tried to come to his lord's defense. In the Tang dynasty, he was ennobled as the "Marquis of Wei" and later in the Southern Song as the "Duke of Wei."

13.

Half Portraits of the Great Sage and Virtuous Men of Old: Yan Yan

Anonymous, Yuan dynasty (1279-1368)
Album leaf, ink and colors on paper, 33.3 x 24.3 cm

Yan Yan (506-443 BCE), a native of Wu who had the style name Ziyou and also was called Yan You or Shu shi ("Master Uncle"), was 45 years younger than Confucius. Among the 72 recognized disciples of Confucius, he is the only known southerner. Famous for his literary skills, he once served as the Minister of Wucheng in the state of Lu (the hometown of Zeng Shen, modern Bixian in Shandong). He educated the people via music and the rites, being famous for his musical abilities and receiving the praise of Confucius. After becoming accomplished in his own right, he returned south and established the Way in southeastern China, making a great contribution to cultural advancement in the Jiangnan region. Known as "Master of the South," he is revered as Yanzi ("Master Yan"). In the Kaiyuan reign of the Tang dynasty, he was ennobled as the "Marquis of Wu," in the Song dynasty as the "Duke of Danyang," and later also as the "Duke of Wu."

14.

Half Portraits of the Great Sage and Virtuous Men of Old: Bu Shang

Anonymous, Yuan dynasty (1279-1368)
Album leaf, ink and colors on paper, 33.3 x 24.3 cm

Bu Shang (507-? BCE), style name Zixia, was born into a poor family but a diligent student. One of the Ten Philosophers among Confucius' disciples, he excelled at literary studies and once taught at Xihe (modern Weinan, Shaanxi) in the state of Wei, serving as the teacher of Marquis Wen of Wei. Bereaving the death of his son, he wept until losing his eyesight, for which he was reprimanded by Zeng Shen. Among Confucius' disciples, the one with the most writings to his name is Bu Shang. Legend has it that *Mao's Version of the Book of Poetry* came from Bu Shang and that *Preface to the Poetry* was also by him. Furthermore, he is recorded as writing "Chapter on Mourning Apparel" in *Rites and Ceremonies* and *Commentary on the I Ching*. Being one of the most dedicated to the Confucian classics, it demonstrates the importance of Bu Shang's status.

15.

Illustrating *The Classic of Filial Piety*

Calligraphy and painting by Gaozong (1107-1187) and Ma Hezhi (ca. 1130-ca. 1170), Song dynasty
Album leaf, ink and colors on silk, 28.8 x 33.7 cm

The Classic of Filial Piety, consisting of eighteen chapters, was reportedly written by the disciples of Zengzi (Zheng Shen, 505-435 BCE) after inquiring with Confucius. It discusses people as belonging to five levels of society, starting with the ruler at the top and ending with commoners at the bottom. It also explains the methods and course of putting filial piety into practice.

The painting here is the first leaf to a "Song Album of *The Classic of Filial Piety* in Painting and Calligraphy," showing Confucius at his residence giving a lecture and Zengzi kneeling before him to ask about filial piety. It appears to have originally been a handscroll with alternating segments of painting and calligraphy that was later remounted due to damage into an album of painting and calligraphy mounted on separate leaves. The texts and images throughout complement each other, the paintings employing various scenes to present the ideas of fully expressing filial piety in different levels of society and the loyal gentleman. It fully manifests the original intent behind its creation as "words for a ruler."

The style of calligraphy in this album is similar to that of Emperor Gaozong but most likely done by a ghostwriter in his Calligraphy Academy. The painting, however, differs from that of Ma Hezhi but is nonetheless a work of the Song dynasty.

16.
The Classic of Filial Piety

Calligraphy and painting by Wen Zhengming (1470-1559) and Qiu Ying (ca. 1494-1552), Ming dynasty
Handscroll, ink and colors on silk, 30.1 x 679.8 cm

Wen Zhengming, a native of Changzhou (modern Suzhou), Jiangsu, was a literati artist who excelled at painting and calligraphy. In the latter, his greatest achievement was in small regular and small semi-cursive script. Qiu Ying (style name Shifu, sobriquet Shizhou), a native of Taicang in Jiangsu, was a professional painter whose style was fine and elegant.

The Classic of Filial Piety, with its emphasis on filial piety among Confucians, has more than 1,800 characters, making it the shortest among the Thirteen Classics of Confucianism. This handscroll departs from the Song dynasty tradition of alternating text and imagery. Here, Confucius is seated on a platform on the right at the beginning as he lectures to his disciples, followed by the eighteen chapters of *The Classic of Filial Piety*. The brushwork is strong and succinct.

According to the colophon by Wen Zhengming dated to the equivalent of 1546, Qiu Ying did this painting after a work by Wang Duan (fl. ca. 1004-1023), an artist of the Northern Song period. After finishing it, the collector Wang Zuobin then asked Wen to write the text in regular script below the illustrations, forming the scroll of painting and calligraphy seen today.

17.
Guqin Forms Through the Ages

Anonymous, Song dynasty (960-1279)
Album leaf, ink on paper, 37.6 x 27.2 cm

The Chinese zither, also known as the "guqin," is one of the oldest plucked instruments in Chinese history. It was already popular at the time of Confucius, and the artist of this album depicts "Fuxi Playing the Guqin," "Shennong Playing the Guqin," and "Shun Playing the Five-Stringed Guqin" to extend its history back to China's legendary rulers. The naming of different forms also reflects the traditional veneration for sages, rulers, and scholars in Chinese culture. This album was originally stored at the Chonghua Palace, the former residence of the Heir Apparent in the Qing dynasty. Traditionally ascribed to a Song dynasty artist, it depicts in monochrome ink the forms of guqin used by rulers and sages through history. At the top of each work is a record with related information.

For this display, "Laozi's Form" and "Confucius' Form" have been chosen. For Confucius, it relates a story known to many: "When in Qi and hearing the imperial music of Shao, he (Confucius) did not notice the taste of meat." The form of the instrument with indentations at either end and its fluid outlines is known as the Confucius type. Commonly seen since the Tang and Song dynasties, it is the most popular since antiquity. The style of this painting, while based on that of the Song dynasty, suggests a copy from the Ming dynasty (1368-1644) instead.

18.

Full Portraits of the Sagacious Gentleman and Virtuous Officials:
Laozi and Confucius

Anonymous, Song dynasty (960-1279)
Album leaf, ink on silk, 28.6 x 21.8 cm

This album in monochrome ink on silk features full portraits of rulers and sages prior to the Five Dynasties period (907-960), ranging from Fuxi to the Tang emperor Dezong (742-805). The painting style is similar to the Song dynasty copy of "Admonitions of the Instructress" in the British Museum, the lines here even more direct and simplified. On display in this exhibit is the seventeenth leaf, which features portraits of Confucius and Laozi. The fine strokes are even, fluid, and strong, the drapery lines with ink washes having a feeling of high antiquity.

"The House of Confucius" in *Records of the Grand Historian* records how the ruler of Lu and Confucius went to Zhou to ask Laozi about the rites and propriety. The author, Sima Qian (?-90 BCE), records Laozi as saying, "I have heard that men of wealth and rank give money as a gift, while men of virtue give a few words. I am not a man of wealth or rank but have been called a man of virtue, so let me give you a few words. 'Those of great intelligence or observational skills bring themselves closer to death by talking about others. Those of great eloquence or learning stir up trouble for themselves by exposing the faults of others. As the younger in a family, one should not think highly of oneself. As a subordinate in office, one should not think highly of oneself.'" This is the origin behind the story of Confucius meeting Laozi.

19.

Illustrated Investigation of Sacrificial Rites at the Temple of the Sage:
Portrait of the Great Sage of All Teachers, Confucius

Gu Yuan (1799-1851), Qing dynasty
Imprint of the Ciyan Hall, 1826, Qing dynasty
18 x 12.5 cm

The portrait of Confucius here is a woodblock print illustration in lines that depicts him with much facial hair and wearing formal official garments. Seated upright, he is also holding a scepter-tablet. Judging from the gesture of his hand and the mouth slightly open, it may be surmised to be an illustration of Confucius "At His Hometown" from *The Analects of Confucius*, which states, "When he was in the ancestral temple or at court, he spoke articulately but with caution."

The object that Confucius holds is described in the "Jade-bead Pendants" section of *The Book of Rites* as follows: "For his memorandum-tablet, the Son of Heaven used round jade; the nobility, a piece of ivory; Great Masters, a piece of bamboo ornamented with fishbone; and officers, bamboo with ivory at the bottom. When he pointed to or drew something for the ruler, he used the tablet. Going before him and receiving an order, he wrote on it. For all these purposes, the tablet was used, and so it was ornamental." According to regulations governing ancient rituals, all members of nobility and the court were required to bring a tablet when having an audience with the emperor, which was used for illustrating or pointing something out as well as taking memos.

This woodblock illustration shows Confucius describing the state of affairs to the ruler in the ancestral temple. The lines for the depiction appear like the gossamer strands of high antiquity, each one even and refined yet strong. On the opposing page are the positions and titles bestowed upon Confucius by emperors from the Zhou to Sui dynasties.

20.

Portraits of Virtuous Sages with Eulogies: The Great Sage of All Teachers, Confucius

Lü Weiqi (1587-1641), Ming dynasty
Imprint of the Chongzhen reign (1628-1644), Ming dynasty
19 x 14 cm

Compiled by Lü Weiqi and printed in the late Ming dynasty, this edition lacks the last stroke in "xuan 玄," a taboo character in the Kangxi reign (1662-1722), suggesting it was printed at that time. Here, Confucius is shown as a stout figure with a Confucian cap. He has heavy facial hair and holds a scepter, sitting upright and looking ahead with a serious and spirited demeanor. The lines are decisive and strong, the style archaic, featuring large areas of ink for the robe folds to create a dramatic visual contrast with flowing white for the drapery lines.

Lü Weiqi (style name Jieru), a native of Xin'an (modern Henan), was a Neo-Confucian in the Ming dynasty and the son of the famous Henan Confucian Lü Kongxue. Lü Weiqi studied Neo-Confucianism since childhood, becoming a Presented Scholar in 1613, serving as a judge in Yanzhou, and being selected as Secretary in the Ministry of Personnel. However, he ran afoul of the notorious eunuch Wei Zhongxian (1568-1627) and resigned to return home, establishing the Zhiquan Lecture Hall there. Later, in the Chongzhen reign (1627-1644), he was restored to office and served as Minister of War in Nanjing. When the rebel leader Li Zicheng attacked Luoyang, Lü Weiqi was captured but did not capitulate, leading to his execution. Lü thus received the posthumous title of Zhongjie for his loyalty and a similar one (Zhongjing) by the following Qing dynasty court.

21.

Illustrated Investigation of Sacrifices at the Temple of the Sage: Learning from Guqin Master Xiang

Gu Yuan (1799-1851), Qing dynasty
Imprint of the Ciyan Hall, 1826, Qing dynasty
18 x 12.5 cm

This text is divided into five fascicles ("juan," or chapters) and records the order promulgated by the Qing court of Confucius, his disciples, and famous Confucians over the ages. It features 144 portraits and short biographies of the figures from the Han to Qing dynasties venerated at temples dedicated to Confucius.

The editor of this text, Gu Yuan (style name Xiangzhou), a native of Changzhou (modern Suzhou), was an Instructor during the Daoguang reign (1821-1850) and a famous bibliophile, printing a large number of books as well. The illustrator of this text was Kong Jiyao (style name Yanxiang, sobriquet Lianxiang), a native of Kunshan in Jiangsu who excelled at engraving bird-and-flower and especially figural subjects. Many of Gu's publications have portrait copies by Kong.

This edition was published in the sixth year of the Daoguang reign (1826) by Gu Yuan's Ciyan Hall. Many illustrated biographies on Confucius through the ages are known as "Illustrated Traces of the Sage." The page here is from the fifth fascicle of this book and entitled "Learning from Guqin Master Xiang," showing Confucius learning to play the "guqin" from the music official Xiangzi. Text and image complement each other, demonstrating the spirit of Confucius striving to understand through dedicated learning. Depicted with lines in this woodblock print, Confucius is seated below a pine tree with his sleeves rolled and plucking the instrument with great concentration.

22.

Illustrated Investigation of Sacrificial Rites at the Temple of the Sage:
Visiting the Musician Chang Hong

Gu Yuan (1799-1851), Qing dynasty
Imprint of the Ciyan Hall, 1826, Qing dynasty
18 x 12.5 cm

Chang Hong (?-492 BCE), a native of Shu in the Eastern Zhou (corresponding to Zizhong County, Sichuan), was a famous scholar and official gifted in various subjects, including astronomical and calendrical studies, music, and music theory. In "Sacrifices to the Heavens and Earth" from *Records of the Grand Historian*, Sima Qian writes that "King Ling of the Zhou consulted Chang Hong on the heavens." Chang was the consultant on heavenly matters and omens of good and bad fortune for the Zhou king.

This is an illustration of Confucius visiting Chang Hong to inquire about music matters took place in the period between the 24th to 25th years of King Jing's reign in the Zhou dynasty (496-495 BCE). The opposing leaf also includes anecdotal textual information to the effect that the famous Chang Hong told others about finding evidence from the appearance of Confucius that corresponded to the features of ancient sages.

23.

Illustrating the School Sayings of the Sage Confucius:
Confucius Asking Laozi About the Rites

Wu Jiamo, Ming dynasty (1368-1644)
Imprint of the Ming dynasty
21 x 13.7 cm

Wu Jiamo in the Ming dynasty based his book here on *Illustrated Traces of the Sage* at Qufu. Compiled, edited, engraved, and printed in 1589, Cheng Qilong (sobriquet Boyangfu) was the illustrator, while Huang Zu of Anhui was responsible for the engraving. Composed of ten fascicles, the first one deals with an illustrated biography of Confucius from when he was born up to his death. With a total of forty illustrations, each has an opposing page of text and relevant sayings. Here, the woodblock illustration is rendered succinctly, the composition even and the lines fluid using rough carving, focusing on the spirited expression of the figure.

Fascicles two to ten deal with the text for *The School Sayings of the Sage Confucius*. As early as Eastern Han dynasty brick illustrations, the subject of "Confucius Asking Laozi About the Rites" was quite common. Related records on this subject appear in "Zengzi Asks" from *The Book of Rites*, the biographies of Laozi and Han Feizi in *Records of the Grand Historian*, *The School Sayings of Confucius*, and *Zhuangzi*.

II. Engravings on Confucius

After Confucius passed away, subsequent rulers and local officials through the ages conferred upon him posthumous titles, made offerings, and renovated the Temple of Confucius, events that were often commemorated and engraved in stone steles. The people who composed and wrote these steles were often notable figures at the time. Over the years, the number of such steles increased and collected to form the famous "Forest of Stone Steles." The "Yi Ying," "Ritual Vessels," and "Shi Chen" steles are all masterpieces of Han dynasty clerical script admired by calligraphers today and serve as important examples to emulate.

24.
Rubbing of the Yi Ying Stele

Anonymous, Han dynasty (206 BCE-220 CE)
Hanging scroll, ink on paper, 191.1 x 88.5 cm

The "Yi Ying Stele" was erected in 153 CE during the Eastern Han dynasty. The text engraved on the original stone records the nineteenth-generation descendant of Confucius, Kong Lin. He had asked the court to follow Han dynasty precedents governing ancestral temples to establish the post of Clerk to be responsible for the ritual vessels at the Temple of Confucius and the ceremonies held there in spring and autumn. After petitions by former Administrator Yi Ying and then Ping, as well as by Wu Xiong and Zhao Jie, Ministers of Education and Works, respectively, Kong He as a descendant of Confucius known for his virtue and learning as well as his filial piety was finally chosen to serve in this position.

The original stele in Qufu, Shandong, is also called the "Kong He Stele" and currently located at the Temple of Confucius there. The engraved text in clerical script is upright and solemn. Later in the Qing dynasty (1644–1911), it was praised by scholars as a classic example of Han clerical script and became a model that most calligraphers studied for this type of writing.

The stele not only mentions the people involved with the Temple of Confucius at the time but also several times the offerings that were made. It describes the nobility of Lu providing money for dog meat and wine as offerings; an ox, sheep, hog, and chicken each provided by the Governor of Henan; and rice by the Chamberlain for the National Treasury. Thus, the stele provides important information on the kind of sacrificial offerings made at the Temple of Confucius in its early years.

25.
Rubbing of the Ritual Vessels Stele

Anonymous, Han dynasty (206 BCE-220 CE)
Hanging scroll, ink on paper, 167.5 x 76.8 cm

The full name of this stele is "Ritual Vessels Stele Made by Han Chi, Han Administer of Lu." It also goes by the names "Han Chi Stele" and "Stele on Renovating Ritual Vessels at the Temple of Confucius." Engraved in 156 CE, it is one of the three major steles at the Temple of Confucius along with those of "Yi Ying" and "Shi Chen." The stele text records how the Administrator of Lu renovated the Temple of Confucius and purchased ritual vessels, contributing funds along with other citizens to engrave and erect a stele to commemorate the event.

This stele is a classic example of Eastern Han engraved calligraphy. The spacing in the characters is complete and the brush movement varied, creating for a style that is fine yet strong as well as robust and majestic. The solemn and upright manner features character forms that are harmonious and steady, providing an overall spirit of detachment as well as beautiful elegance and solemnity. Students of Han dynasty clerical script often take this as a model of freedom and ease, the stele subsequently having a major influence on later generations of calligraphers.

This stele mentions the Yan clan of Confucius' mother and the "Qiguan 亓 官" clan of his wife. While known as the Qiguan clan today, *General Records* of the Song dynasty and encyclopedias on surnames of the Ming and previous periods use "Bingguan 并官" instead.

26.

Rubbing of the Shi Chen Stele

Anonymous, Han dynasty (206 BCE-220 CE)
Hanging scroll, ink on paper, 170 x 82 cm

The "Shi Chen Stele" is located in the Temple of Confucius at Qufu. Engraved on both sides of the stone, the back is known as the "Shi Chen Stele Back." Engraved in the first year of the Jianning year of Emperor Lingdi in the Eastern Han dynasty (168 CE), it records how Shi Chen, the Administrator of Lu, renovated the Temple of Confucius. The front of the stele, called "Shi Chen Stele Front," was engraved in the following year. It mentions how Shi Chen made offerings to Confucius upon becoming an official there and how he petitioned to have sacrifices performed for Confucius every spring and autumn.

The style of calligraphy on the front and back of the stele is similar, appearing as if coming from the same hand and exhibiting very little wear. The character forms are tight and reduced but with extended slanting angular strokes. The arrangement of the characters is even and the original brush method gentle and reserved. The solemn and profound force here has a deep and heavy sense of archaism. The method is also exacting, having both structure and feeling to make it an excellent example of Eastern Han clerical script.

The stele back mentions a descendant of Confucius, Kong Biao, who was Governor of Hedong. He is the subject of the "Kong Biao Stele," the style of which served as the predecessor of Yan Zhenqing's (709-785). He was also the younger brother of Kong Zhou, the father of Kong Rong (153-208). All members of the same clan, the talent and prominence of Confucius' descendants are readily apparent.

27.

Rubbing of the Lu Temple of Confucius Stele from the Huangchu First Year

Anonymous, Wei dynasty (220-265)
Hanging scroll, ink on paper, 183 x 90.7 cm

The "Lu Temple of Confucius Stele," also known as the "Kong Xian Stele," is now preserved at the Temple of Confucius in Qufu. Carved in the first year of the Huangchu reign in the Wei dynasty during the Three Kingdoms period (220 CE), it records how Kong Xian, a 21st-generation descendant of Confucius, was bestowed with the title of "Marquis Revering the Sage (Zongsheng hou)," conducted sacrifices to Confucius, and made repairs to the Temple of Confucius.

The character forms in the engraved text here follow those of Han dynasty clerical script, the style of calligraphy powerful yet reserved, the characters dense and vigorous as well. The "bones" of the strokes are forceful with a majestic spirit. The brushwork is even and archaic, comparable to pins and needles, serving as a forerunner for the regular script that emerged in the Six Dynasties period. A representative of Wei clerical script, this stele was regarded by the ancients as the premier example of engraved calligraphy from the Wei dynasty.

The descendants of Confucius inherited bestowed titles, beginning with Kong Teng in the ninth generation, who was awarded as "Lord Offering Sacrifices (Fengsi jun)" by Emperor Gaozu of the Han dynasty. The title most often bestowed in the Western and Eastern Han dynasties was "Praising Perfection Marquis (Baocheng hou)," which in the Wei dynasty was changed to the aforementioned "Marquis Revering the Sage." The one that lasted the longest was "Duke Fulfilling the Sage (Yansheng gong)" bestowed in the Northern Song period, which survived until 1935. In modern times, the Nationalist government in Nanjing awarded Kong Decheng, a 77th-generation descendant of Confucius, the position of "Official for Offering Sacrifices (Fengsi guan)."

28.

Rubbing of the Li Zhongxuan Stele on Repairing the Temple of Confucius

Anonymous, Eastern Wei dynasty (534-550)
Hanging scroll, ink on paper, 213.6 x 83.3 cm

This stone stele, also known as the "Li Zhongxuan Stele," was engraved in the third year of the Xinghe reign in the Eastern Wei dynasty (541) and is now preserved at the Temple of Confucius in Qufu. The header features characters in claw-like seal script that reads, "Stele of the Temple of Confucius in Lu." The main text records how Li Ting, Prefect of Yanzhou, renovated the crumbling walls of the Temple of Confucius. He also repaired the statute of Confucius inside, having portraits of Confucius' ten major disciples done as well. The stele text is engraved in regular script with many elements of clerical script. Moreover, it is interspersed with large and small seal script as well as draft clerical. The large number of writing forms reflects a trend common at the time.

This stele is the earliest record of imagery made of Confucius and his "Ten Wise Disciples." In ancient times, his image at the Temple of Confucius was in sculptural form. Later, in the Ming dynasty, Emperor Taizu (r. 1368-1398) ordered the sculptures be replaced with sacrificial tablets during reconstruction of the Temple of Confucius, because it was felt they did not adequately convey their spirit of the figures. Emperor Shizong in the Jiajing reign (1522-1566) then ordered the removal of Confucian sculptures all over the country to be replaced with tablets, which is one reason why so few images of him in the round survive at the various Temples of Confucius today.

29.

Rubbing of Pei Xiaozhi's Record for Inscribed Gates at the Temple of Prince Wenxuan

Pei Ping (fl. 8th c.), Tang dynasty
Hanging scroll, ink on paper, 144 x 71 cm

This stele, also known as "Record of Renovating the Three Gates at the Temple of Prince Wenxuan," "Record of the Three New Gates at the Temple of Prince Wenxuan," and "Stele for Renovating the Gates at the Temple of Prince Wenxuan," is now located at the Temple of Confucius in Qufu. It records how in 773 Meng Xiujian, Prefect of Yanzhou, and Pei Youxiang, District Magistrate of Qufu County, had new gates built for the Temple of Confucius in Qufu. Pei Xiaozhi, Vice Director of the Bureau of Sacrifices and Attendant Censor, was responsible for composing the text and Pei Ping did the calligraphy and the stele header. The main text is in clerical script, the characters regulated and thorough, the brush method handsome in appearance with wavy strokes strong and upright. The thickness of the strokes varies greatly, revealing the inclusion of clerical methods found in regular script during the Tang dynasty.

After Confucius passed away, many rulers over the years conferred upon him honorific titles as a sign of respect. Of all the periods in Chinese history, the variations of titles given to Confucius were greatest during the Tang dynasty. Emperor Taizong referred to him as "Father of Teaching (Xuanfu)," Emperor Gaozong further added the title "Grand Master (Taishi)," and Wu Zetian used "Duke of the Grand Way (Longdao gong)." In 739, Confucius was posthumously ennobled with the title of "Prince of Teaching and Propagation (Wenxuan wang)," thereby beginning the history of his elevation to the ranks of "princedom."

30.

Rubbing of the Record on Renovating the Temple of Prince Wenxuan in the Jianlong Third Year

Anonymous, Song dynasty (960-1279)
Hanging scroll, ink on paper, 183.6 x 79 cm

This stele is now preserved at the "Stele Forest" in Xi'an. In the third year of Emperor Taizu's Jianlong year

(962), early in the Song dynasty, Wang Yanchao (914-962) had this stele erected. The contents describe how Emperor Zhaoxuan in 904, late in the Tang dynasty, had the "Imperial University and the Classics in Stone" moved from the old district of Chang'an to the new city, making this the earliest known record of moving the Stone Classics in the Tang dynasty.

The running script in the stele here is a classic example of the Northern Song court style of calligraphy. The header with an inscription for "Sagacious Prince for Teaching and Propagation (Wenxuan)" was later engraved in 1008 (the first year of Emperor Zhenzong's Dazhong Xiangfu reign). The person behind this stele was Wang Yanchao (style name Desheng), whose biography is found in History of the Song. A prominent general of the late Five Dynasties to early Song dynasty, he was ennobled as Duke of Bin and awarded the post of Director of the Department of State Affairs. In addition to this stele, he also engraved a copy of the "Hall Stele of the Temple of Confucius" by Yu Shinan from the Tang dynasty that was destroyed by fire several times.

The Stele Forest at Xi'an preserves the legacy of the Four Books and Five Classics of the Imperial University in Chang'an. Along with the Temple of Confucius, these are the two places in China with the largest concentration of steles related to Confucius.

III. Confucianism Through the Ages

Confucius perhaps can be regarded as the person who has influenced China the most. The impact of his thought can be found over the course of Chinese history, including the sayings of various philosophers (such as Xunzi and Mencius), the numerous annotations and commentaries for the Chinese Classics, the sayings of many renowned Confucians who have upheld the spirit of Confucius, and the large number translations into Manchu for the Four Books and Five Classics in the Qing dynasty. In addition, the imperial plaques presented to temples dedicated to Confucius throughout the land show the unparalleled respect and honor bestowed upon Confucius by rulers through the ages.

31.

"Exemplar Teacher for a Myriad Generations" from the Imperial Brush

Shengzu (1654-1722), Qing dynasty
Horizontal scroll, ink on paper, 109.2 x 393 cm

Emperor Shengzu, who went by the personal name Aisin Gioro Xuanye, is better known by his reign name, Kangxi. An admirer of Confucian thought and Neo-Confucianism, he also spent much time doing calligraphy, in which he copied from the ancient modelbooks of the Jin and Tang dynasties. He later received instruction from Shen Quan (1624-1686) and learned the running script of Dong Qichang (1555-1636), which he combined with the styles of Song and Yuan dynasty masters.

In *Grand Occasion of the Imperial Visit to Lu*, Kong Yuqi, a 67th-generation descendant of Confucius, recorded the 1684 visit by the Kangxi emperor on his southern inspection tour to the hometown of Confucius. The emperor also awarded a handscroll with the characters for "Exemplar Teacher for a Myriad Generations" in praise of Confucius. In the following year, an engraving was made and rubbings presented to temples dedicated to Confucius all over the country.

This work, originally an artifact from the family mansion of Confucius' descendants, features character forms that are solid with brushwork steady and having an even force. The lifting of the brush, however, was quick and decisive, making it an excellent example of the Kangxi emperor's large-character calligraphy done

with a suspended wrist. The layering of the strokes is clear and the traces of the brush precise and detailed, suggesting it is the original upon which other plaques from the brush of Kangxi are based at various Temples of Confucius.

32.

The Four Tenets of Yichuan

Shen Quan (1624-1684), Qing dynasty
Hanging scroll, ink on silk, 170 x 51.7 cm

Shen Quan (style name Zhenrui; sobriquets Yitang and Chongzhai), a native of Huating (modern Shanghai) in Jiangsu, was a Presented Scholar of the Shunzhi reign (1644-1662) who served to the post of Vice Minister of Rites. Good at poetry, he excelled at calligraphy as well, his scholarship and character likewise outstanding.

The "Four Tenets" here are those of "Master Yichuan," referring to the Song dynasty Neo-Confucian philosopher Cheng Yi (1033-1107) and based on the "Yan Yuan" section of *The Analects of Confucius*. In it, Confucius said to "deny thyself and return to the Rites," from which the four disciplines of morality formed: "Look not at anything inconsistent with the Rites," "Hear not anything inconsistent with the Rites," "Speak not of anything inconsistent with the Rites," and "Do not do anything inconsistent with the Rites."

Shen Quan first studied the calligraphy of Dong Qichang (1555-1636) and in his later years achieved the depths of Mi Fu's (1052-1108) style. He was once summoned to the inner court by the Kangxi emperor to discuss calligraphy of the past and present. Shen's style fully reflects the phenomenon of "particular brilliance in imitation during the Kangxi and Yongzheng reigns." Shen did this work at the age of 54 with characters beautifully refined and slanting to the side, the spirit harmony of the characters much influenced by that of Dong Qichang.

33.

Imperial Poetry Done After Reading *Extended Meaning of the Great Learning*

Zhang Zhao (1691-1745), Qing dynasty
Hanging scroll, ink on silk, 172 x 80 cm

Zhang Zhao (style name Detian; sobriquets Jingnan and Tianping jushi), a native of Huating (modern Shanghai, Songjiang), was a Presented Scholar of 1709 who served to the post of Minister of Justice and was posthumously bestowed with the name Wenmin. Learned in interpreting the Classics and law, he was also gifted at music and especially calligraphy. He first learned the style of Dong Qichang (1555-1636) and then went back to the manners of Mi Fu (1052-1108) and Yan Zhenqing (709-785), developing an angular yet expansive quality in his brushwork with a majestic and powerful force that has a modern touch much admired.

Zhen Dexiu (1178-1235), the author of *Extended Meaning of the Great Learning*, was a famous Southern Song Neo-Confucian who followed the thought and studies of Zhu Xi (1130-1200). His book was promoted by later generations for advocating the way of statesmanship and uprightness in office, the Kangxi emperor in the Qing dynasty describing it as the "Orthodoxy of strength and brightness." It was required reading for rulers in the Qing dynasty.

This scroll is a transcription of poetry written by the Qianlong emperor (Gaozong, 1711-1799). The characters are dense and the arrangement evenly halted. The style is a mix of regular and running script, suggesting the styles of Yan Zhenqing from the Tang and Zhu Xi of the Song.

34.

Forest of the Changes by Master Jiao in Clerical Script

Yang Xian (1819-1896), Qing dynasty
Hanging scroll, ink on paper, 132.3 x 63.9 cm

Yang Xian (style name Jianshan; sobriquets Miaoweng and Chihong canweng), a native of Gui'an (in modern Zhejiang), was a Provincial Graduate of 1855 who served as Prefect of Changzhou. He was good at poetry and prose while excelling at calligraphy, his clerical official script said to have followed the past and paved the way for the future.

The author of *Forest of the Changes by Master Jiao* is Jiao Yanshou (style name Gong; also said to be named Gong with the style name Yanshou). He lived in the state of Liang in the Western Han period (in what is now the southern part of modern Shangqiu, Henan). Generally speaking, the book is in the form of four-character sentences, the contents summarizing his understanding of *The Book of Changes (I Ching)*. It is thought that Jing Fang (77-37 BCE), the progenitor of the "Jing Fang *I Ching*" method of prognostication, was a disciple of Jiao.

This scroll, done in 1891 when Yang Xian was 73 years old by Chinese reckoning, is an excerpt from this text in Han clerical script. The style of the calligraphy derives from the "Ritual Vessels Stele," but the application and lifting of the brush, the variation between wet and dry ink, and the expansive quality of the characters are all in Yang's own manner. The force is decisive and spirited in a style of his own.

35.

Transcription from *Mencius*

Kang Youwei (1858-1927), Qing dynasty
Hanging scroll, ink on paper, 158 x 44 cm

Kang Youwei (original name Zuyi; style name Guangxia; sobriquets Changsu and Gengsheng), a native of Nanhai in Guangdong, was an initiator of the failed "Reform Movement of 1898" in the late Qing dynasty, which later became known in history as the "Hundred Days' Reform." In calligraphy, Kang studied the "Eulogy at Stone Gate" and was the author of *Two Oars for the Vast Boat of Art*. In calligraphy, he looked down upon modelbooks and advocated steles.

This work, donated to the National Palace Museum by the sisters Huang Li-jung and Huang Wen-ju, is a transcription from the chapter on "Fully Explore the Mind" in *Mencius*. It reads, "Myriad things are within us all. What greater delight is there than to be sincere in self-examination? Act with vigor and nothing will be closer than seeking the realization of benevolence." The idea is that everything exists within us all, so we just need to find the path of goodness with sincerity and effort. Reflecting on ourselves, we will naturally think of others.

The brush movement in this work is fluid and the brushwork "astringent." The characters are tight but expansive, the momentum precipitous and the force powerful. The overall manner is majestic and strong without attention to details, which is a feature of Kang Youwei's style of calligraphy.

36.

Excerpt from *The Family Sayings of Confucius* in Cursive Script

Shen Zengzhi (1852-1922), Republican period
Hanging scroll, ink on paper, 141.2 x 76.1 cm

Shen Zengzhi (style name Zipei; sobriquet Xunzhai [or Yikan]; late sobriquet Meisou; alternate name Yigong), a native of Jiaxing in Zhejiang, was a Presented Scholar of 1880 who served to the post of Provincial Administration Commissioner of Anhui. A scholar of vast learning, he focused in calligraphy on studying

modelbooks in his early years and later combined Han clerical, Northern stele script, and draft cursive into a single style of his own. He also did small landscapes bearing a light and elegant harmony.

This work is a selection of two pieces in semi-cursive script from *The Family Sayings of Confucius*, which records the words of Confucius to his disciples and events in his life. They are "Book 11, Observing (the Duke of) Zhou" and "Book 18, Yan Hui," in which importance is attached to the quality not quantity of talk. This scroll incorporates the method of calligraphy from the "Cuan Baozi Stele," emphasizing variations to the strokes as they rise and fall in detail, the curving manner also appropriate for a force that flies sharply about. The gestures are settled and archaic with slanting strokes reaching outwards for a topsy-turvy approach, the highly personal manner here suggesting Shen's late style.

37.
The Great Learning in Manchu

Pu Ru (1896-1963), Republican period
Mounted, ink on paper, 20.5 x 43.2 cm

Pu Ru, better known by his style name Hsin-yu, also had the sobriquet Xishan yishi. A grandson of Yixin, Prince Gong, he was a member of the Qing imperial family and lived in Beijing. He delved into poetry, the Classics and history, and the arts of painting and calligraphy since childhood. He excelled at the latter two, beginning by copying works of the old masters. Pu Ru and Chang Dai-chien were known as "Chang of the South and Pu of the North." Pu later moved to Taiwan and became one of the most important traditional painters in modern Taiwan.

This work, entrusted to the National Palace Museum from the Cold Jade Hall, is a selection from *The Great Learning* written in official Manchu script, starting from the passage for "Way of the Great Learning" to "There is no example of it." The signature reads, "The above is a passage from the Classic, (signed) Pu Ru." The Manchu rulers of the Qing dynasty firmly upheld the principle of "Confucian orthodoxy as the ruling orthodoxy." They placed much emphasis on studying Confucian Classics to lay a theoretical foundation for their rule of China. The Kangxi emperor (1662-1722) even translated into Manchu the Four Books of Confucianism, which became teaching materials for the daily imperial colloquium on the Chinese Classics. The Confucian notions of cultivating the self, maintaining one's family, ruling the country, and spreading peace throughout the land also strongly influenced Manchu thought and culture.

Also included here is a Manchu-Chinese transliteration of *The Great Learning from Imperial Translation of the Four Books* printed in the Qing dynasty during the Qianlong reign (1736-1795).

38.
Illustrated Explanations as a Mirror for the Emperor

Zhang Juzheng (1525-1582), Ming dynasty
Handwritten Imperial Household edition, Qing dynasty (1644-1911)
Illustrated by Shen Zhenlin (fl. 19th c.), Qing dynasty
53.5 x 53 cm

Zhu Yijun (1563-1620), the Ming emperor Shenzong better known by his reign name Wanli, assumed the throne at the age of ten. Zhang Juzheng and other officials who assisted him collected 117 examples of rulers in Chinese history, composing texts and having each one illustrated to form a picture book to cultivate the young boy into a virtuous ruler.

This is a handwritten painted version from the Qing dynasty court. Shen Zhenlin (style name Fengchi), a native of Wuxian (modern Suzhou, Jiangsu), was a painter who served at the court during the Xianfeng and Tongzhi reigns (1851-1874). He specialized in figural and portrait painting, in which he achieved a high reputation.

The painting here depicts the story of "Passing Through Lu to Make Offerings to the Sage," in which the Han dynasty emperor Gaozu in 195 BCE returned to the capital after quelling the Rebellion of Ying Bu. Passing by Qufu, the hometown of Confucius, he held sacrifices of the highest order for the sage, including the Three Sacrificial Offerings (ox, sheep, hog). He also bestowed upon the ninth-generation descendant of Confucius, Kong Teng, the title of "Lord Offering Sacrifices" to specifically attend to the sacrifices for Confucius. This event would become a precedent among future rulers for making offerings to Confucius.

39.

Illustrated Explanations of Renovating Various Buildings in Taiwan Prefecture

Jiang Yuanshu (1738-1781), Qing dynasty
Imprint of the Qianlong reign (1735-1796), Qing dynasty
32.3 x 41.1 cm

Jiang Yuanshu (style name Zhongsheng, sobriquet Xiangyan), a native of Changshu in Jiangsu, was a Provincial Student of 1759 who served as the Prefect of Taiwan from 1775 to 1778. From 1776 to 1777, he also was in charge of General Surveillance in the Taiwan Circuit, making many contributions to the island during his tenure as an official.

This work on "Illustrations of Ritual Vessels at the Temple of Confucius" comes from *Illustrated Explanations of Renovating Various Buildings in Taiwan Prefecture*. In 1776, Jiang noted, "All the vessels used at the Temple of Confucius in Taiwan Prefecture are made of lead-tin bronze, which is of humble quality. The 'dou,' 'bian,' 'fu,' and 'gui' vessels also do not conform to the norms, and many are missing." Therefore, "I, Yuanshu, carefully consulted Confucian regulations and selected artisans in Suzhou to establish a workshop, purchase bronze, create a foundry, and cast instruments for music and the rites. I spent more than 10,000 cash and had them shipped to Taiwan." In the following year, he wrote an inscription and Directors Chen Zuolin (fl. ca. 18th-19th c.) and Lin Chaoying (1739-1816) engraved a stone stele, which is now at the Temple of Confucius in Tainan and an important early document on the veneration of Confucius in Taiwan.

IV. Illustrating the Classics

Starting from the Western Han period, the ideas of Confucius became increasingly emphasized by rulers. The government promoted Confucian ethics and virtues for cultivating moral character and adjusting and maintaining the five norms of interpersonal relationship in Chinese society: ruler and subject, father and son, elder and younger brother, husband and wife, and between friends. This idea served as a spiritual guide for scholars to help govern the country and as an important force for maintaining social order. Figures that Confucius admired such as the courageous Bian Zhuangzi, ancient verses in *The Book of Poetry*, and stories about Confucius' disciples are among the Confucian contents that have been illustrated in painting and print over the centuries.

40.
Bian Zhuangzi Stabbing a Tiger

Anonymous, Song dynasty (960-1279)
Handscroll, ink and light colors on silk, 39 x 169.1 cm

Bian Zhuangzi, a Grand Master from the city of Bian in the state of Lu (1027-250 BCE), was renowned for killing two tigers in one move. When the state of Qi heard of this, they dared not attack Lu. The story that this handscroll illustrates can be found in *Strategies of the Warring States* and "Exemplary Biography of Zhang Yi" in *Records of the Grand Historian*. The main point of the story is similar to the fable of the snipe and an oyster, in which both struggled to hold onto each other and refused to yield, resulting in their easy capture by a passing fisherman.

In the story here, an ox had died on the grass and two tigers came to fight over the corpse. Bian Zhuangzi took a sword to kill the tigers, but an advisor stopped him, saying the tigers would fight until one died and the other was wounded and could be easily killed. Bian took his advice, waited, and easily finished off the surviving tiger. At the end of the scroll are six figures responsible for the sword, staff, and other implements of Bian. The painting bears no seal or signature of the artist, but the fine yet strong brushwork for the struggling tigers and the courage of Bian Zhuangzi are all in an archaic manner of the Song dynasty, creating for a dynamic scene.

In "Book 14, Xian Asks" of *The Analects of Confucius*, Confucius answers a question posed by Zilu, citing the courage of Bian Zhuangzi. Both Zilu and Bian Zhuangzi were natives of the city of Bian, illustrating the idea of filial piety, military valor, or some customs of the area.

41.
Illustrating the "Odes of Bin"

Painting and calligraphy attributed to Wang Zhenpeng (fl. first half of 14th c.) and Ke Jiusi (1290-1343), Yuan dynasty
Handscroll, ink and colors on silk, 53.3 x 893.6 cm

Bin, in the area north of Mt. Qi, was the place where the Zhou ancestors established their dynasty. When King Cheng (?-1021 BCE) assumed the throne as a child, Duke Zhou (?-1032 BCE) served as his regent and wanted the king to understand the importance of agriculture and sericulture (silk production) to the state and to care for the livelihood of the people throughout the year. As a result, he wrote the "Odes of Bin" to proclaim the tradition of focusing on agriculture by Hou Ji and Duke Liu, ancestors of the Zhou dynasty rulers.

This handscroll painting illustrates "Seventh Month" from the "Odes of Bin" and is the longest of the poetry among the fifteen odes of states in *The Book of Poetry*, compiled by Confucius, and dealing throughout with agricultural matters. In the total of eight sections, it first describes food and clothing, followed by farming and sericulture, and then finally discusses hunting and autumn harvest in preparation for winter storage. The handscroll is colored with blue-green hues, and each section is accompanied by a text written to the side for reference.

The inscriptions and colophons make reference to Wang Zhenpeng and Ke Jiusi as the painter and calligrapher, respectively, of the scroll. However, the painting already reveals the influence of Qiu Ying's (ca. 1494-1552) style, suggesting instead a Suzhou forgery of the sixteenth century or later with the names of these two Yuan artists added to it.

42.

Window of Broken Pottery

Zhao Mengfu (1254–1322), Yuan dynasty
Handscroll, ink and colors on silk, 27.1 x 100.5 cm

Zhao Mengfu (style name Zi'ang, sobriquet Songxue daoren) was gifted at writing poetry and prose with pure lyricism. He also promoted revivalism in painting and calligraphy in the manner of the Tang and Song dynasties, becoming a model for later generations.

The painting illustrates the story of Confucius' disciples. One day, Zigong visited the residence of Yuan Xian, who lived in a humble hut with mulberry wood supports and a window made from broken pottery. It illustrates the idea of how a true gentleman takes joy in the Way and not material possessions, the story also appearing in "Exemplary Biographies of the Disciples of Zhongni (Confucius)" in *Records of the Grand Historian*. Duanmu Ci, style name Zigong, was a native of Wei and 31 years younger than Confucius. He became wealthy as a merchant and went on to serve as a statesman in Lu. On the other hand, Yuan Xian, a native of Song 26 years younger than Confucius, was poor but took joy in studying the Way in reclusion.

The painting here is done without texture strokes for the mountains and landforms, featuring only precise outlines filled with blue-green coloring. The brushwork for the drapery lines of the figures is fluid yet powerful in the archaic manner of the Tang dynasty. In the lower right corner of the painting is the character "suo 索" from the "Thousand-Character Essay" used as an accession number by Xian Yuanbian (1525–1590) in the Ming dynasty. There is also an inscription of his that reads, "Remounted at the Tianlai Pavilion in the eighth lunar month during autumn in the 31st Jiajing year of the Ming (1558)" and his record for the "original price: 50 taels."

Yuan Xian (515–? BCE), a native of Lu with the style name Zisi and also known as Yuansi, was one of the earliest disciples of Confucius. When Confucius was serving in Lu as a judge, Yuan Xian managed his household affairs. After Confucius passed away, Yuan Xian reportedly quit office and went into reclusion. In "Xian Asks" from *The Analects of Confucius*, Yuan Xian is recorded as asking Confucius about the subjects of shame and benevolence. "Yong Ye" in the same book also suggests that he quit the rank of minister with a salary of 900 bushels of grain but was encouraged by Confucius that he could still be of benefit to others around him. In *The Family Sayings of Confucius*, Yuan Xian is said to be "pure and faithful, poor but taking joy in the Way." He was later ennobled by Emperor Xuanzong in the Tang dynasty as "Earl Yuan" and as "Marquis of Rencheng" by Emperor Zhenzong in the Song dynasty.

Essay

The Forms of Confucius in Painting and Confucian Themes in Calligraphy

Sung-feng Wu

Abstract

Over the course of Chinese history, nobody has exerted as much influence as Confucius. Even after more than two millennia, the ideas of Confucius continue to serve up to this day as benchmark values for weighing propriety in Chinese cultural circles. The forms of Confucius and vestiges of veneration for him by rulers in the past can still be found in many places today. In addition to the Four Books and Five Classics, as well as stories in historical books, there are also paintings used in the past to enlighten people, educate them about human relations, and highlight the achievements of Confucius. Because much emphasis was placed on subjects related to Confucius, they were often engraved in stone by later generations, which is why they have been preserved to a greater degree in this medium.

Nowadays, among the subjects related to Confucius found in Chinese art, there are two issues of particular interest. The first one is the multiple appearances of Confucius. In other words, what did Confucius actually look like? The second is peripheral forms of textual evidence. It goes without saying that scholars trained in Confucian thought would compose writings and do calligraphy related to it. To reflect their reverence for the importance of Confucian ideas, the texts and calligraphy of these scholars were often the best of their time. This is not to mention the plaques that rulers over the ages presented in their own writing, which were often done not just out of respect but also to promote themselves as enlightened sages in the orthodox tradition of Confucius. This essay addresses the above two topics to introduce how later generations portrayed and venerated Confucius, from time to time presenting works with traces of the imagery and ennoblement of Confucius.

Teacher Exemplar
for a Myriad Generations

Confucius in Painting, Calligraphy,
and Print Through the Ages

國立故宮博物院
NATIONAL PALACE MUSEUM

國家圖書館出版品預行編目 (CIP) 資料

萬世師表：書畫中的孔子 / 吳誦芬編輯 . -- 初版 . --
臺北市：故宮 , 民 106.06
面；　公分
ISBN 978-957-562-790-4（平裝）
1.（周）孔丘　2. 學術思想　3. 博物館特展

121.23　　　　　　　　　　　　　　　　106009691

萬世師表　書畫中的孔子

Teacher Exemplar for a Myriad Generations
Confucius in Painting, Calligraphy, and Print Through the Ages

Issuer: Jeng-yi Lin

Editor: Sung-feng Wu

Proofreaders: Fang-ju Liu, Yanchiuan He, Chi-fa Chuang, Ji-gang Zeng

Essay & Entry Authors: Sung-feng Wu

English Translator: Donald E. Brix

Assistant Editor: Shiu-Lan Kang

Publisher: National Palace Museum

Add: 221, Zhishan Road, Section 2, Shilin District, Taipei, Taiwan, R. O. C.

Tel: +886-2-28812021

Fax: +886-2-28821440

http://www.npm.gov.tw

Designer & Printer: Red & Blue Color Printing Co.

9, Lane 327, Zhongshan Road, Zhonghe District, New Taipei City, Taiwan, R. O. C.

Tel: +886-2-22401141

Distributor: NPM's Art Development Fund (National Palace Museum)

Add: 221, Section 2, Zhishan Road, Shilin District, Taipei City 111, Taiwan, ROC

Tel: +886-2-28812021 (ext. 68977)

Postal remittance account: 19606198

Email: service@npmeshop.com

First printing: June 2017

Price: NT$860

ISBN: 9789575627904

GPN: 1010600832

發　行　人：林正儀

主　　　編：吳誦芬

監　　　修：劉芳如、何炎泉、莊吉發、曾紀剛

文 字 撰 述：吳誦芬

英 文 翻 譯：蒲思棠（Donald E. Brix）

行 政 編 輯：康綉蘭

出　版　者：國立故宮博物院

地　　　址：臺北市士林區至善路二段 221 號

電　　　話：（02）2881-2021

傳　　　真：（02）2882-1440

網　　　址：http://www.npm.gov.tw

製 版 印 刷：紅藍彩藝印刷股份有限公司

地　　　址：新北市中和區中山路 2 段 327 巷 9 號

電　　　話：（02）2240-1141

總　代　理：國立故宮博物院故宮文物藝術發展基金

地　　　址：臺北市士林區至善路 2 段 221 號

電　　　話：（02）2881-2021 分機 68977

郵 政 劃 撥：19606198

電 子 信 箱：service@npmeshop.com

出 版 日 期：中華民國 106 年 6 月　初版一刷

定　　　價：新臺幣 860 元

國 際 書 號：9789575627904

統 一 編 號：1010600832